中国金融科技创新监管工具
China FinTech Innovation Regulatory Facility

白皮书
White Paper

中国人民银行金融科技委员会
FinTech Committee of the People's Bank of China

中国金融出版社

责任编辑：肖　炜　董梦雅
责任校对：孙　蕊
责任印制：程　颖

图书在版编目（CIP）数据

中国金融科技创新监管工具白皮书／中国人民银行金融科技委员会著.
—北京：中国金融出版社，2020.12
ISBN 978 – 7 – 5220 – 0928 – 5

Ⅰ.①中… Ⅱ.①中… Ⅲ.①金融—科学技术—金融监管—研究
报告—中国 Ⅳ.①F830.2

中国版本图书馆 CIP 数据核字（2020）第 240347 号

中国金融科技创新监管工具白皮书
ZHONGGUO JINRONG KEJI CHUANGXIN JIANGUAN GONGJU BAIPISHU

出版
发行 中国金融出版社

社址　北京市丰台区益泽路 2 号
市场开发部　（010）66024766，63805472，63439533（传真）
网上书店　http：//www.chinafph.com
　　　　　　（010）66024766，63372837（传真）
读者服务部　（010）66070833，62568380
邮编　100071
经销　新华书店
印刷　保利达印务有限公司
尺寸　169 毫米×239 毫米
印张　7.25
字数　55 千
版次　2021 年 1 月第 1 版
印次　2021 年 1 月第 1 次印刷
定价　38.00 元
ISBN 978 – 7 – 5220 – 0928 – 5
如出现印装错误本社负责调换　联系电话(010)63263947

前　言

近年来金融科技蓬勃发展，信息技术与金融业务深度融合，已成为金融业高质量发展的重要驱动力。金融科技创新在为金融发展注入新活力的同时，也使风险隐患更隐蔽、更复杂、更多变，给金融监管的及时性、有效性和包容性带来新挑战。如何做好金融科技创新监管，处理好安全与发展的关系，协调好金融与科技的关系，在守住风险底线的前提下，给真正有价值的创新预留充足发展空间，已成为金融管理面临的重要课题。

为贯彻党的十九届四中全会和中央经济工作会议精神，落实《金融科技（FinTech）发展规划（2019—2021年)》，人民银行研究设计包容审慎、富有弹性的创新试错容错机制，划定刚性底线、设置柔性边界、预留充足发展空间，着力打造符合我国国情、与国际接轨的金融科技创新监管工具（以下简称创新监管工具），积极构建机构自治、社会监督、行业自律、政府监管"四位一体"的金融创新安全防线，努力营造守正、安全、普惠、开放的金融创新发展环境，加快健全具有高度适应性、竞争力、普惠性的现代金融体系，为服务实体经济、防范金融风险、深化金融改革注入新动能。

　　为系统全面刻画创新监管工具，积极稳妥推动包容审慎监管新模式落地实施，加快构建具有中国特色的金融科技监管框架，人民银行金融科技委员会特编制本白皮书。本书包含中文版、英文版两部分，从监管框架、运行机制、实施规程、穿透式分析方法等方面依次展开，多角度、全景式对创新监管工具进行系统展示，为我国金融科技监管工作提供依据。

Preface

In recent years, FinTech has been flourishing, and the deep integration of information technology and financial services has become an important driving force for the high-quality development of the financial industry. While FinTech innovation injects new vitality into financial development, it also makes potential risks more concealed, more complex and more variable, bringing new challenges to the timeliness, effectiveness and inclusiveness of financial regulation. How to properly regulate FinTech innovation, handle the relationship between security and development, and reserve sufficient development space for truly valuable innovation on the premise of guarding the bottom line of risks has become an important subject to be resolved in financial regulation.

In order to implement the spirit of the Fourth Plenary Session of the 19th CPC Central Committee and the Central Economic Work Conference, as well as "The Development Program of FinTech (2019—2021)", the People's Bank of China has researched and designed an inclusive, prudent and flexible innovation trial and error tolerance mechanism, drawn a rigid bottom line, set flexible boundaries and reserved sufficient space for development, striving to create Innovation Regulatory Facility for FinTech (hereinafter referred to as "Innovation Regulatory Facility") in line with China's national conditions and international standards. The People's Bank of China actively builds a four-in-one financial innovation safe line combining institutional autonomy, social supervision, industry self-discipline and government monitoring, endeavors to create upright, safe, inclusive, and opening development environment for financial innovations, speeds up the improvement of a modern financial system with a high degree of adaptability, competitiveness and inclusiveness, and injects new energy into serving the real economy, preventing financial risks and deepening financial reforms.

The white paper is specially made to help portray the Innovation Regulatory Facility systematically and comprehensively, actively and safely promote the implementation of the inclusive and prudent new mode of regulation, speed up the construction of a FinTech regulatory framework with Chinese characteristics. The paper contains Chinese and English version, from the aspects of regulatory framework, operating mechanisms, implementation protocols, penetrating analysis method, systematically introduces Innovation Regulatory Facility from multiple perspectives and panoramic views, and provides a basis for China's FinTech regulatory efforts.

目　录

CONTENTS

一、重要意义

（一）构建金融转型升级新引擎

当前，全球新一轮科技革命和产业变革蓬勃发展，金融供给侧结构性改革深入推进，金融创新与技术变革融合演进，金融数字化转型已成为行业发展的大势所趋。出台创新监管工具能够加速金融监管模式从被动监督向主动服务蝶变，强化监管对创新应用的引领、护航和孵化作用，引导金融机构、科技公司等市场主体把握好数字化转型的历史机遇期，积极探索运用新一代信息技术优化产品形态、服务渠道、经营模式和业务流程，推动技术创新成果更好在金融领域落地应用，助力金融服务降低成本、提升效益，增强金融数字化转型能力和核心竞争力，为我国金融业高质量发展提速赋能。

（二）应对数字金融发展新挑战

随着数字技术更新换代的速度持续加快，金融与科技相互融合、螺旋迭代的趋势越发明显，金融新产品和新业态大量涌现。金融创新初期往往面临商业模式不够清晰、风险隐患不易辨识等问题，针对性监管细则和风控措施难以及时出台。创新监管工具引入社会监督力量，打造包容审慎的创新试错容错机制，既有利于在依法依规、保障消费者权益的前提下，释放科技创新活力，深挖金融应用潜能；又有利于金融管理部门在缩小版真实市场环境中更好把握创新本质与风险实质，加速研究出台针对性监管举措，有效纾解数字金融发展带来的新挑战。

（三）打造金融风险防控新利器

在金融科技时代，金融服务渠道网络化、形态数字化，金融业务更加虚拟、边界逐渐模糊，不同业务互相关联渗透，传统金融风险传导的时空限制被打破，风险规模和传播速度呈指数级增长，给金融风险防控带来新挑战。创新监管工具积极探索数字化监管实践，基于监管科技手段打造多层次、立体化金融科技风控体系，有助于实现对创新风险的多渠道态势感知、综合性评估分析和差异化预警处置，强化跨市场、跨业态、跨区域风险联防联控能力，筑牢金融科技创新风险"防火墙"，为打赢防范化解金融风险攻坚战提供有力支撑。

（四）开拓金融创新监管新局面

技术是中性的，本身没有好坏之分，应用得当能给金融发展注入新的动力，应用不当也可能引发新的风险。然而，为应对金融科技背景下机构综合经营、业务多层嵌套、风险交叉传导给金融稳定和金融市场带来的冲击，部分国家采取"一刀切"的严监管措施，主观或客观上导致市场主体科技创新能力受到束缚、活力难以释放。创新监管工具秉持包容审慎监管理念，把创新与安全作为一个有机整体统筹考虑，既管控好技术创新应用带来的风险，又不过度附加安全措施而影响创新效率，在实践中探索既要稳定又要发展的金融科技监管双赢新模式，推动金融科技创新与安全双轮驱动、协同并进，着力提升金融监管的专业性、统一性和穿透性。

二、监管框架

（一）基本原则

一是持牌经营。金融科技的本质是金融，金融业务持牌经营是申请测试的基本条件。科技公司在满足通用安全要求的前提下，可直接申请测试，涉及的金融服务创新和金融应用场景须由持牌金融机构提供。科技公司既可联合金融机构共同申报，也可单独申报后结合应用场景选择合作金融机构。**二是合法合规**。安全是不可逾越的底线和红线。金融机构应依法合规，管控好新技术创新应用带来的风险隐患，确保创新不偏离正确方向。**三是权益保护**。秉承以人民为中心的发展理念，建立健全与金融创新发展相适应的消费者权益保护机制，切实保障金融消费者合法权益。**四是包容审慎**。践行柔性监管理念，既加强审慎监管，确保不发生系统性金融风险，又增强监管包容性，释放金融创新发展动能。

（二）设计思路

"工欲善其事，必先利其器"。创新监管工具探索建立更具穿透性与专业性的创新监管框架，提升金融科技创新监管效能。**一是划定刚性底线**。以现行法律法规、部门规章、基础规范性文件等为准绳，从业务合规、技术安全、风险可控等方面明确守正创新红线。**二是设置柔性边界**。运用信息披露、公众监督等柔性监管方式，让人民群众参与金融科技治理，为金融科技创新营造适度宽松的发展环境。**三是预留创新空间**。在守住安全底线的基础上包容合理创新，支持市场主体享有平等参与创新机会与条件，最大限度地运用现代信息技术赋能金融提质增效，给真正有价值的创新预留足够空间。

（三）监管理念

1. 破解"一管就死、一放就乱"困局，提高监管适用性。在金融科技时代，金融服务更多元，业务交叉嵌套、风险形势更严峻，传统创新监管模式在一定程度上出现"失灵"。金融管理部门迫切需要在保护金融消费者合法权益的前提下，既鼓励从业机构主动创新，又能及时发现并规避创新缺陷与风险隐患。人民银行打造新型创新监管工具，旨在处理好安全与创新的关系，针对我国百花齐放的金融科技创新形势，探索出一条既能守住安全底线，又能包容合理创新、高度适配我国国情的金融科技监管之路，破解创新监管面临的"一管就死、一放就乱"困局，规范和引导金融科技健康有序发展。

2. 摒弃"一刀切"简单模式，增强监管包容性。从历史经验来看，适当的监管力度是发挥金融监管效能的关键，力度过小易导致大量欺诈产品涌入市场，进而损害金融消费者合法权益；反之，力度过大易导致从业机构合规成本过高，从而降低创新活力。新型创新监管工具选择什么样的监管力度，是金融管理部门考量的重要因素。在设计之初，我们秉持包容理念，主动摒弃"一刀切"模式，积极探索更具引导性、启发性和激励性的新型柔性监管方法，增强政府部门、创新主体和社会公众之间的信息交流和良性互动，打造符合新事物内在发展规律的监管模式，营造包容的金融科技创新环境。

3. 引入"多元联动"公众监督机制，提升监管有效性。我国金融机构数量众多、服务创新方兴未艾，传统"政府监管＋机构自治"模式面临较大挑战。引入更多外部力量参与监督是优化创新监管模式的有效手段。考虑到数以亿计的社会公众是金融产品的最终服务对象，他们对创新应用的安全性与便利性更有发言权。为此，创新监管工具引入了公众监督机制，充分发挥不同社会主体作用，让金融消费者深入了解创新产品功能实质、潜在风险和补偿措施，更好地保障其合法权益；让新闻媒体发挥雷达作用，对创新产品安全性、合规性和合法性进行监督；让第三方专业力量参与事前把关，全面评估安全防护措施的可靠性和有效性。通过上述多元联动监督机制，推动构建"协同共治"的金融科技创新监管新模式，提升监管有效性。

4. 设置创新应用"刚性门槛"，强调监管审慎性。金融科技发展不能走互联网金融的老路，既要重视柔性监管，也要重视审慎监管。科技驱动的金融创新在一定程度上是向未知领域的探索，风险与变数如影随形，应对不当可能加剧不确定性，甚至引发系统性风险。为此，新型创新监管工具强调审慎监管，力求设置刚性门槛。从金融角度来说，坚持金融科技的本质是金融，严格落实金融持牌经营原则，严防打着"金融科技"的旗号从事非法集资、金融诈骗等违法犯罪活动。从科技角度来说，明确风险底线和安全标准，建立风险动态监测感知、高效处置的风控体系，保障真正有价值的科技新成果能够得到充分测试和迭代完善，最终为金融创新注入科技动力。

（四）治理体系

创新监管工具充分调动社会各方积极性，打造机构自治、公众监督、行业自律和政府监管"四位一体"的金融科技治理体系。**一是机构自治**。金融机构落实创新管理主体责任，加强风险内控和自我约束，主动接受公众监督和行业自律，建立健全投诉响应、应急处置、风险补偿和保险赔付机制，切实保障用户合法权益。**二是公众监督**。社会公众作为治理体系的中坚力量，通过多种渠道全面了解产品信息，及时发现可能存在的风险隐患，并以建议、投诉、申诉等方式实现对金融科技创新"质效"的充分监督。**三是行业自律**。行业协会在治理体系中发挥桥梁纽带作用，配合政府部门做好投诉受理、自律约束、宣贯培训等工作，为管理要求落地实施提供有力支撑。**四是政府监管**。金融管理部门作为治理体系的主导者，建立健全监管协调与监督实施机制，确保各项管理措施落地。

三、运行机制

（一）安全管理机制

金融安全是国家安全重要组成部分，发展金融科技应将保障金融安全作为不可逾越的底线和红线。金融科技是技术驱动的金融创新，其风险是动态变化的，具有较高突发性和不可预测性。为更好防控创新风险，摸清金融服务测试运行状况，便于及时出台有针对性的监管细则，创新监管工具坚持包容审慎原则，严守安全底线，建立健全涵盖创新应用事前、事中、事后全生命周期安全管理机制，全面筑牢金融科技创新风险防线（见图1）。

1. **事前审慎把关。一是以业务合规为前提，**通过内部机构审计、外部专业评估、征求管理部门意见等方式，确保金融创新不突破法律法规、部门规章、基础规范文件等红线要求，严防以"创新"为名突破现行业务规则的虚假创新。**二是以技术安全为保障，**对照创新安全通用规范、个人金融信息保护规范等金融行业标准进行评估，严防存在技术漏洞和风险隐患的应用参与测试，全面提升创新应用的标准符合性与安全性，确保信息技术安全、合理、规范地应用于金融领域。**三是以风险可控为目标，**督促申请机构建立健全风险内控制度，落实风险管理主体责任，完善风险补偿、应急处置、服务退出等机制，切实保障用户资金和信息安全，坚决守住不发生系统性金融风险的底线。

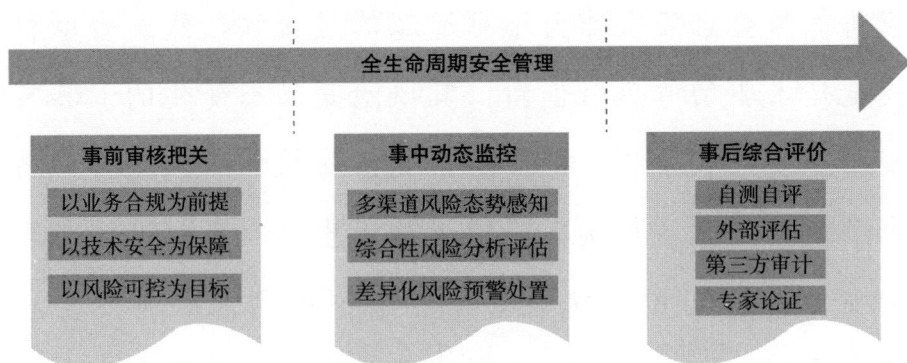

图1 安全管理机制

2. **事中动态监控。**建立金融科技创新管理服务平台，运用数字化监管手段持续动态监测创新应用运行状况，及时定位、跟踪、预防和化解风险隐患。**一是多渠道风险态势感知。**加强与网信、公安、工信等部门合作，建立涵盖金融机构、科技公司、行业协会、第三方专业机构和政府部门的协同机制，推动跨行业、跨部门、跨领域风险信息共享。采用机构报送、接口采集、自动探测等方式，基于人工智能、大数据等技术动态感知金融科技应用风险态势。**二是综合性风险分析评估。**提取风险特征信息，将风险归类分级，形成风险数据仓库。通过模型分析、专家评议等方式，准确评估风险影响范围和危害程度，深入分析不同风险特征间的关联关系，及时发现风险趋势与潜在隐患。**三是差异化风险预警处置。**建立创新风险综合防控机制，推进差异化风险预警和高效应急处置。指导测试机构履行风险防控主体责任，借助第三方专业支撑能力，凝聚金融业内外合力，共建风险联防联控机制，严格做到问题早发现、风险早预警、漏洞早补救。对于短期内难以补救的风险漏洞，需要及时发布风险提示，采取综合性风险补偿措施；对存在重大问题的创新应用，应及时阻断并退出测试。造成损失的，测试机构须通过风险拨备资金、保险计划等进行赔偿，切实保障消费者合法权益。

3. 事后综合评价。综合采用自测自评、外部评估、第三方审计、专家论证等方式，从创新价值、服务质量、合法合规、数据安全、风险防控等方面，对提出申请结束测试的创新应用进行综合评价，评估创新应用是否履行声明书承诺、是否惠民利企、是否满足监管要求、是否商业可持续，及时发现并消除潜在隐患，防止创新风险外溢。**一是自测自评**。申请机构通过系统测试、内部审计等方式，组织开展机构内部评估工作，形成自评报告。**二是外部评估**。通过国家统一推行的金融科技技术产品通用安全认证等方式，对创新应用进行全生命周期持续动态安全评定。**三是第三方审计**。通过注册会计师审计等方式，对创新应用声明书相关承诺落实情况进行评估。**四是专家论证**。申请机构组织业务、技术、安全、自律等相关领域外部权威专家组成专家组，在自测自评基础上，结合外部评估、第三方审计情况进行综合评审论证。

（二）创新服务机制

习近平总书记指出，创新是引领发展的第一动力。创新监管工具贯彻党中央、国务院关于建设服务型政府的精神，坚持寓监管于服务、以服务促创新的理念，推动监管模式从被动监督向主动服务转变，积极打造创新试错容错与辅导优化机制，强化产用对接、政企协同与供需撮合，为市场主体提供全方位、立体式、专业化的监管服务支撑，为金融科技创新厚植茁壮成长沃土（见图2）。

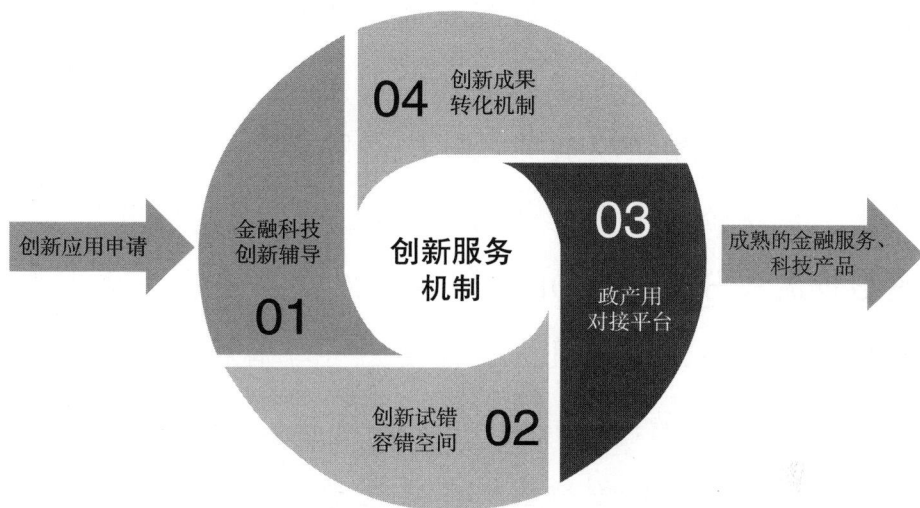

图2 创新服务机制

1. 开展金融科技创新辅导。金融管理部门组织成立专业辅导团队，提供"一对一"的专业化监管辅导，提升创新应用安全合规、惠民利企水平。**在申请辅导方面，**辅导团队与申请机构保持深度交流，从合规性、风险防控、消费者权益保护等方面指导其持续滚动优化创新。对于基础较好的，辅导其完善申报材料；对存在重大问题的，支持其更换选题。申请周期视项目自身情况存在差异，符合条件项目最终均可进入测试。**在业务透视方面，**借鉴业务流程建模（BPM）、统一建模语言（UML）等分析工具，从资金流、数据流、合作关系三个维度辅导申请机构精准识别风险实质，引导金融机构、科技公司更好守正创新。**一是资金链式分析法**

（CCA）。通过对资金流转过程的穿透式分析，剖析关键节点资金用途，厘清全链条资金来源与流向流量，识别资金截留、挪用、空转等风险，严防资金脱实向虚违规使用，保障金融服务真正为实体经济"输血供氧"。**二是数据流式分析法（DFA）**。通过对数据全生命周期的梳理刻画，追踪金融机构、科技公司与消费者间的数据流向和使用情况，界定数据的所有权、使用权、收益权、管理权，评估创新应用在数据采集、使用过程中是否合法合规且获得用户充分授权。对于涉及数据多方使用的，引导创新主体通过多方安全计算、同态加密、特征提取等技术在保障数据安全前提下，实现数据有序共享和融合应用。**三是合作关系分析法（CRA）**。运用背景调查、核心业务逻辑分析等手段，梳理各参与机构间责权分工情况，确保金融科技创新的商业背景真实、业务资质有效、商业模式可持续。

2. 构建创新试错容错空间。 创新是一种探索性的实践，风险和挑战在所难免，要在维护金融稳定与消费者权益前提下，营造"允许出错、及时纠错、快速改错"的创新氛围。创新监管工具构建具有"容错"能力的测试空间，在严防创新风险外溢的基础上，支持市场主体在真实市场环境中对创新应用的理论原型、技术选型、业务模式进行完整业务链条实践与测试，及时发现并弥补潜在风险隐患，有效验证创新价值，通过反复测试、充分打磨快速打造出既满足市场需求又符合监管要求的优质产品服务。

3. 搭建政产用对接平台。创新监管工具充分发挥缩小版真实场景"一端连市场、一端连政府、一端连用户"的优势，深度激活创新要素与资源，协同赋能金融科技创新发展。**在产用对接方面，**通过经验交流、案例分享、联合攻关、同业合作等方式推动金融机构与科技公司加强对接协作，实现金融机构应用需求与科技公司产品供给的高效匹配，提升科技创新成果转化应用效率。**在政企协同方面，**金融管理部门与市场主体之间通过会议研讨、辅导交流、窗口指导等方式不断加强良性互动，在互动中明确创新目标与发展方向，引导金融科技守正创新与安全应用。**在供需撮合方面，**通过信息披露、投诉监督等措施，畅通供需双方交流渠道。金融消费者可以更好地提出意见建议、表达核心诉求；创新主体可以更好地掌握用户需求、研发硬核产品。通过以上措施，强化政产用深度交流与直接对话，形成产业各方相互促进、顺畅衔接的良性循环，为金融高质量发展注入新动能。

4. 完善创新成果转化机制。**一是通过标准化手段增强创新成果生命力**。组织成立专项标准工作组，不断总结测试运营经验，引导测试机构建立健全企业标准体系，积极参与行业标准、国家标准制定，通过标准化手段把好安全关口、卡紧应用标尺、系牢合规准绳，以高标准确保高质量，以高标准聚合知识、技术、人才、数据等要素，实现企业发展的新旧动能转换，逐渐构建质量和品牌优势，不断增强金融科技创新成果生命力。**二是搭建展示平台提升创新成果影响力**。定期或不定期总结风险可控、惠民利企的优秀创新成果，提炼最佳创新实践经验，依托行业协会、产业联盟、联合实验室等平台，通过编发优秀案例库、举办展会论坛、发布产品测评报告和选型指引等方式，提升创新成果示范性和影响力，加快优秀成果转化落地。**三是强化政策扶持降低创新成果转化成本**。用好政府和市场"两只手"，在充分发挥市场配置资源决定性作用的同时，更好地发挥政府引导作用，推动加大对优秀创新项目的政策与资金支持力度，拓宽企业融资渠道、降低科技创新成本、分散产品研发风险，激发市场主体内生发展动力，共同构建金融科技产业发展良性生态。

（三）信息披露机制

信息披露是保障金融消费者合法权益、强化金融市场主体自我约束的有效手段，对促进金融市场的安全、稳健和高效运行至关重要。创新监管工具按照党中央、国务院关于深化"放管服"改革、优化营商环境有关精神。借鉴告知承诺制等新举措，综合运用声明公示、管理登记、用户明示等创新声明方式，多措并举建立覆盖创新应用全生命周期的信息主动披露、全程公开和主动承诺机制，简化测试申请流程、释放市场主体创新活力，提升信息披露的时效性、透明度与可信度，为金融科技创新风险防范、提升创新监管效率提供有力支撑（见图3）。

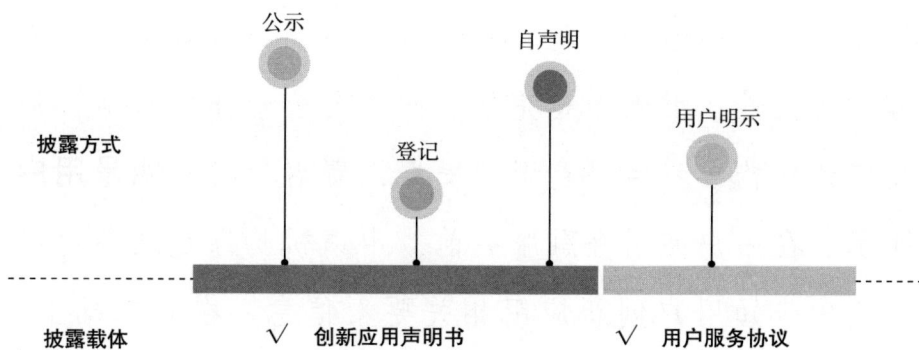

图3　信息披露机制

1. 信息披露载体。**一是声明书。**作为公示、登记、

自声明等信息披露方式的载体，主要包含创新应用基本信息、服务信息、创新性说明、评估报告、风险防控、投诉响应等要素。**二是服务协议书**。作为用户明示的载体，包含创新应用功能服务、责权关系、风险补偿、数据授权等主要信息。金融消费者可通过服务协议书全面了解创新应用功能实质，在充分知情前提下使用金融服务，有效防范因信息不对称带来的消费纠纷等问题。

2. 信息披露方法。**一是公示**。通过声明书向社会公众公开创新应用要素信息，使人民群众及时了解创新真实情况、识别潜在风险并提出改进建议。**二是登记**。申请机构按要求向金融管理部门登记创新应用信息。金融管理部门可有效评估潜在风险，更快出台针对性监管规则。**三是自声明**。申请机构通过官方网站、实体网点等线上线下渠道对创新应用进行自声明，并就自声明内容的真实性、准确性和完整性向社会公众作出承诺，强化申请机构自我监督意识，提振消费者信心。**四是用户明示**。在用户使用金融服务前，申请机构通过服务协议书明确告知用户创新应用相关要素信息。在此基础上，基于金融科技创新管理服务平台，建立覆盖创新应用全生命周期的信息披露机制，让各相关方及时、准确地掌握创新应用最新情况。

（四）权益保护机制

金融消费者是金融业务最终服务对象，规范金融创新主体行为、维护公平公正市场环境、保护金融消费者合法权益是金融科技创新监管的重要目标。合理有效的权益保护机制有助于提振金融消费者对金融市场的信心，增强其使用创新服务、参与创新设计的意愿。创新监管工具通过打造声明公示平台、完善风险补偿机制等一揽子措施，多管齐下引导和规范创新主体行为，保障消费者合法权益，促进金融科技创新健康可持续发展。

图4　权益保护机制

1. **知情与自主选择权。一是信息易于获得。**督促申请机构通过官方网站、微博、APP、实体网点等多元化渠道，运用公示、自声明、用户明示等多种方式进行创新声明，提供丰富的信息触达途径，提升披露信息的可得性。**二是内容真实全面**。对金融科技创新应用的功能服务、潜在风险、补偿措施、投诉机制等进行全面披露，提升声明内容的真实性和完整性。**三是语言通俗易懂**。使用简单、明确、无歧视性且不违反公序良俗的语言，对专业术语、行业背景等进行必要介绍和解释说明，使金融消费者能够轻松看懂声明信息。通过以上措施，让金融消费者全面了解创新应用，并可结合实际自主选择与自身需求相匹配的金融服务，更好地保障其知情与自主选择权。

2. 信息安全权。引导申请机构遵循"用户授权、最小够用、专事专用、全程防护"原则，加强数据全生命周期安全管理，建立健全信息安全长效防控机制，充分评估潜在风险，把好信息安全关口，严防数据泄露、篡改、损毁与不当使用。**在数据采集时**，通过授权协议等方式明示用户数据采集和使用目的、方式以及范围，获取用户授权后方可采集。**在数据存储时**，综合运用加密存储、访问控制、安全审计等措施，强化数据安全与隐私保护能力，降低数据泄露风险。**在数据使用时**，建立数据可信共享与融合应用机制，在不归集、不共享原始数据前提下，仅向外提供脱敏后计算结果，推动数据更好赋能金融创新。**在服务退出时**，按照国家及金融行业相关规范要求做好数据清理、隐私保护等工作。

3. **财产安全和依法求偿权。**财产安全关乎金融消费者的切身利益。既要打好防范和抵御风险的有准备之战，也要提前准备化险为夷、转危为安的应对措施，为金融创新上好财产安全"双保险"。**在财产保护方面，**督促申请机构落实国家和金融管理部门有关要求，完善资金安全管理机制，丰富风险防范手段，采取严格的内控措施和严密的监控手段，有效保障消费者财产不受损失，切实做到未雨绸缪，防患于未然。**在依法求偿方面，**明确风险责任认定方式，设立消费者快速赔付渠道，配套风险拨备资金、保险计划等补偿措施，切实维护消费者合法权益。对非客户自身责任导致的资金损失，承诺提供相应补偿，切实做到"亡羊补牢"。

4. **监督建议权。**建立多层次消费者投诉建议机制，畅通投诉建议受理渠道，更好地解决争议与纠纷。**一是做好机构投诉**。申请主体作为处理投诉建议的责任主体，通过线上线下渠道向公众公开投诉方式和处理机制，在时限内对社会公众投诉建议进行处理反馈。**二是抓好自律投诉**。行业自律组织建立健全自律投诉机制，密切跟进被投诉机构的投诉意见处理进展，并视情况组织调解。**三是落实政府监督**。对行业自律组织调解失败的，金融消费者可向金融管理部门提出申诉。金融管理部门应及时进行调查、核实和反馈，切实保障消费者合法权益。

四、实施规程

　　不以规矩，无以成方圆，金融科技创新离不开行之有效的规则规范保驾护航。人民银行深入剖析新技术金融应用风险本质与客观规律，积极研究制定既利于金融科技创新发展、又能满足金融治理需要规则规范，逐步建成纲目并举、完整严密、互为支撑的金融科技监管基本规则体系。依托国家统一推行的认证体系，推动规则规范落地实施，着力提升金融科技守正创新能力与综合治理水平。其中，《金融科技创新应用测试规范》（JR/T 0198—2020）是金融科技创新管理的基本规则，从实施层面对创新测试全生命周期进行规范，明确声明书格式、测试流程、风控机制、评价方式等方面具体要求，为金融管理部门、自律组织、金融机构、科技公司等开展金融科技创新实践提供共同遵循的依据和准则。该规范具体内容如下。

（一）测试声明

1. 声明要求

（1）**真实准确**。声明应遵循"真实、准确、完整、及时"要求，不得虚假记载、误导性陈述、遗漏或拖延公开创新应用信息。

（2）**简洁易懂**。声明应使用简明易懂的语言，对专业术语、专业背景、行业知识等进行必要介绍和解释说明，便于用户了解创新应用信息。

（3）**信息一致**。声明应采用中文文本，如同时采用外文文本的，应保证各文本的内容一致。文本之间产生歧义的，以中文文本为准。

（4）**合法合规**。声明应符合法律法规关于国家秘密、商业秘密、个人信息保护、知识产权保护有关规定。

（5）**长期保存**。应对声明材料进行妥善留存，留存时间为自通过公示之日起至少20年。

（6）**全面声明**。本文件没有规定，但不声明相关信息可能导致用户出现重大误解、产生错误判断的，申请机构应将此类信息予以及时声明。

2. 声明方式

（1）公示

1）公示时间和渠道。申请机构应在创新应用向用户正式提供服务前至少 25 个工作日申请公示，公示期为 5 个工作日。金融科技创新应用在公示期间发生重大变更的，申请机构应及时更新信息并重新申请公示。

2）公示形式。应以金融科技创新应用声明书形式进行公示。声明书应包含创新应用基本信息、服务信息、合法合规性评估、技术安全性评估、风险防控、投诉响应机制、承诺声明等要素，详见"3. 声明要素"章节。

（2）登记

1）登记时间和渠道。申请机构应在创新应用完成公示后的 5 个工作日内申请登记。

2）登记形式。应以金融科技创新应用声明书形式进行登记。

（3）自声明

1）自声明时间和渠道。申请机构应在完成登记后、向用户正式提供服务前，在官方网站、微博、APP、实体网点等线上线下渠道显著位置进行自声明，就自声明内容的真实性、准确性、完整性向公众作出承诺。

2）自声明形式。应以金融科技创新应用声明书形式进行自声明。

（4）用户明示

1）用户明示时间和渠道。申请机构应在用户签约时，明确告知用户声明书中要求明示的要素。

2）用户明示形式。应以服务协议书等形式进行用户明示，并提供用户查询、下载的渠道。

3. 声明要素

（1）创新应用基本信息

1）创新应用编号。创新应用编号由 26 位字母和数字组成，分三部分：申请机构营业执照上的统一社会信用代码（18 位）、提交创新应用声明书的年份（4 位）和项目编号（4 位），中间用"－"分隔。适用于公示、登记、自声明和用户明示（见表 1）。

示例：某申请机构的统一社会信用代码为 91210200TK0QE7GT5L，则该机构 2019 年第五个创新应用声明的编号应为 91210200TK0QE7GT5L－2019－0005。

表1　创新应用编号组成

第一部分	第二部分	第三部分
统一社会信用代码（18位）	提交创新应用声明书年份（阿拉伯数字，4位）	项目编号（阿拉伯数字，4位，由0001开始累加）

2）创新应用名称。创新应用名称应简洁明了、易于理解，原则上不超过20字。适用于公示、登记、自声明和用户明示。

3）创新应用类型。包括金融服务、科技产品两种类型。适用于公示、登记、自声明和用户明示。

4）机构信息

①统一社会信用代码。应填写申请机构营业执照上的统一社会信用代码。适用于公示、登记、自声明和用户明示。

②全球法人识别编码。如有，应填写申请机构的全球法人识别编码（LEI）。适用于公示、登记、自声明和用户明示。如无，可不填。

③机构名称。应填写申请机构营业执照上的名称。适用于公示、登记、自声明和用户明示。

④持有金融牌照信息。如有，应填写参与创新应用项目中持牌金融机构的金融牌照信息，包括牌照名称、发证机关、牌照编号。适用于公示、登记、自声明和用

户明示。如无，可不填。

⑤拟正式运营时间。应填写创新应用拟向用户正式提供服务的时间。描述方式为 yyyy 年 mm 月 dd 日，如 2019 年 02 月 27 日。适用于公示、登记和自声明。

⑥技术应用。应简要描述所使用的现代化信息技术，以及该技术为金融服务提供的功能。原则上不超过 150 字。适用于公示、登记和自声明。

⑦功能服务。应描述创新应用为用户所提供的主要服务、功能信息，并说明研发与运维过程是否有第三方机构参与，明确其参与环节和工作内容。原则上不超过 200 字。适用于公示、登记、自声明和用户明示。

⑧创新性说明。应描述项目在技术应用或金融服务上的创新点，明确创新应用的创新性。适用于公示、登记、自声明和用户明示。

⑨预期效果。应简要描述创新应用上线后预计产生的社会效益、市场价值等，原则上不超过 50 字。适用于公示、登记、自声明和用户明示。

⑩预期规模。应简要描述创新应用上线后的预期规模，包括但不限于用户数、交易量、交易额等量化指标，原则上不超过 50 字。适用于公示、登记、自声明和用户明示。

（2）创新应用服务信息

1）服务渠道。应描述申请机构向用户提供创新应用的通道或途径。适用于公示、登记、自声明和用户明示。

2）服务时间。应描述创新应用可正常完成服务的时间范围。不同的服务渠道可有不同的服务时间。适用于公示、登记、自声明和用户明示。

3）服务用户。应描述创新应用的适用人群。适用于公示、登记、自声明和用户明示。

4）服务协议书。应填写用户使用本创新应用时需要了解并同意相关内容。适用于公示、登记、自声明。

（3）合法合规性评估

1）评估机构。应填写评估机构的中文全称。适用于公示、登记、自声明和用户明示。

2）评估时间。应填写评估机构出具合法合规性评估材料的时间。描述方式为 yyyy 年 mm 月 dd 日，如 2019 年 02 月 27 日。适用于公示、登记、自声明和用户明示。

3）有效期限。应填写合法合规性评估材料的有效期。描述方式为 X 年，如 3 年。适用于公示、登记、自声明和用户明示。

4）评估结论。应简要描述合法合规性评估结论，原则上不超过100字。适用于公示、登记、自声明和用户明示。

5）评估材料。应提供创新应用的合法合规性评估材料。评估材料包括但不限于评估依据、评估方法、评估分析、评估结论。适用于公示、登记和自声明。

（4）技术安全性评估

1）评估机构。应填写评估机构的中文全称。适用于公示、登记、自声明和用户明示。

2）评估时间。应填写评估机构出具技术安全性评估报告的时间。描述方式为 yyyy 年 mm 月 dd 日，如 2019 年 02 月 27 日。适用于公示、登记、自声明和用户明示。

3）有效期限。应填写技术安全性评估报告的有效期。描述方式为 X 年，如 3 年。适用于公示、登记、自声明和用户明示。

4）评估结论。应简要描述技术安全性评估结论，原则上不超过100字。适用于公示、登记、自声明和用户明示。

5）评估材料。应提供该创新应用的技术安全性评估材料。评估材料包括但不限于以下内容：评估依据、评估方法、评估分析、评估结论。适用于公示、登记和自声明。

（5）风险防控

1）**风控措施**。应描述创新应用可能存在的威胁用户资金或敏感信息安全潜在风险，并说明针对风险采取的防范措施。适用于公示、登记、自声明和用户明示。

2）**风险补偿机制**。应描述创新应用可能存在的潜在风险，并说明针对风险采取的防范措施。适用于公示、登记、自声明和用户明示。

3）**退出机制**。应描述创新应用的退出创新测试的机制。退出机制应能够在创新应用正常退出或因特殊情况导致非正常退出时，确保数据安全，防范资金失窃风险，实现平稳退出。退出机制包括但不限于退出条件、退出方案、执行部门、资金流转等内容。适用于公示、登记和自声明。

4）**应急预案**。应提交创新应用的应急预案。应急预案应能提高应对突发事件的综合管理水平和应急处置能力。应急预案包括但不限于突发事件的定义与分级、处置原则、预防与预警机制、应急保障、应急培训与演练等内容。适用于公示、登记和自声明。

（6）投诉响应机制

1）机构投诉

①投诉渠道。应填写接收用户投诉的渠道信息，包括但不限于营业网点地址、通信地址、电话、传真、电子邮箱、官方网站、微博、APP 等。适用于公示、登记、自声明和用户明示。

②投诉受理与处理机制。应填写投诉受理与处理机制相关内容，包括但不限于受理部门、受理时间、处理流程、处理时限等信息。适用于公示、登记、自声明和用户明示。

2）自律投诉

①投诉渠道。如有，应填写接收自律投诉的渠道信息，包括但不限于营业网点地址、通信地址、电话、传真、电子邮箱、官方网站、微博、APP 等。适用于公示、登记、自声明和用户明示。

②投诉受理与处理机制。应按照行业自律要求，填写自律投诉受理与处理机制相关内容，包括但不限于受理部门、受理时间、处理流程、处理时限等信息。适用于公示、登记、自声明和用户明示。

（7）承诺声明

申请机构应对所申报创新应用，就金融科技创新应用声明书内容真实性、准确性、完整性进行承诺声明，并加盖机构公章。

4. 声明流程

声明主要包含以下流程：

（1）**准备**。申请机构应严格遵循现行法律法规、部门规章和规范性文件，按照《金融科技创新安全通用规范》（JR/T 0199—2020），建立健全内部管控、安全防控、应急处置、服务退出等机制，采取风险拨备资金、保险计划等措施最大限度地补偿风险事件给用户造成的损失，切实保障金融消费者合法权益。科技公司作为申请机构时，须由持牌金融机构为其提供科技产品的金融场景支撑。

（2）**申请**。申请机构应按要求填写金融科技创新应用声明书，通过金融科技创新管理服务平台提交申请。

（3）**受理**。组织测试的金融管理部门（以下简称测试管理部门）、自律组织①对申请机构报送声明书的规范性、完整性、公平性、内容合理性进行核实。如通过，自律组织应对创新应用上线后可能产生的影响进行评估，形成评估材料提交测试管理部门；如未通过，回到（1）。

---

① 自律组织受测试管理部门委托开展金融科技创新测试的声明书审核、公示等的相关自律工作。

（4）公示。测试管理部门、自律组织应将声明书在金融科技创新管理服务平台进行公示。

（5）监督。在公示期内，申请机构应就声明书的合法合规性、合理性等接受公众监督。如公众对公示内容有意见，可向自律组织反映，到（6）；如无意见，则公示通过，到（7）。

（6）意见处理。自律组织应及时将公众意见汇总并反馈给申请机构。申请机构收到反馈意见后，应与意见反馈方妥善沟通并达成一致，并于5个工作日内将公众意见处理情况报送自律组织。

（7）评估。自律组织应对意见处理情况进行分析研判，将有关情况报测试管理部门核实确认。如评估未通过，则回到（1）。

（8）登记。评估通过后，申请机构应按要求进行登记。相关科技产品应在登记之前提交外部权威专业机构出具的JR/T 0199—2020标准符合性证明材料。

（9）自声明。完成登记后，申请机构应按本文件进行自声明。

（10）用户明示。申请机构在用户签约时，应按本文件进行用户明示。

（11）变更。在声明要素发生变更时，申请机构应重新填报声明书，并按流程重新进行声明。

（二）测试运行

1. 风险内控。申请机构应建立健全风险内控制度，落实风险管理的主体责任，定期开展创新应用安全审计与评估，明确各岗位、人员的管理责任，完善风险事件应急处置与责任追究机制。对第三方机构参与创新应用设计开发、安全评估等环节的，应严格落实国家和金融行业相关管理要求，确保不让渡风险管理责任。

2. 风险监测。自律组织应按照《金融科技创新风险监控规范》（JR/T 0200—2020）要求，利用金融科技创新管理服务平台持续动态监测创新应用运行状况，加强风险外部感知，及时定位、跟踪、预防和化解创新应用测试运营过程中的风险隐患，并定期向测试管理部门报告。申请机构应将创新测试期间的重要事件、操作记录、系统日志等及时报送自律组织。

3. 风险处置。申请机构应建立健全综合性风险处置与补偿机制，推进差异化风险预警和高效应急处置，切实做到问题早发现、风险早暴露、漏洞早补救；对于短期内难以补救的风险漏洞，及时采取综合性风险补偿措施；对存在严重安全隐患或发生重大风险事件的创新应用，应及时报告测试管理部门和自律组织，视情况退出测试。造成损失的，应通过风险拨备资金、保险计划等进行赔偿，切实保障金融消费者合法权益。

4. 投诉建议

（1）机构投诉

1）投诉渠道

申请机构应建立投诉机制，通过官方网站、微博、APP、营业网点等线上线下渠道显著位置，向公众公开长期有效的投诉电话、传真、电子邮箱、通信地址等。

2）投诉流程

投诉受理与处理主要包含以下流程：

①投诉受理。申请机构应及时受理用户投诉。

②投诉处理。申请机构应充分了解投诉情况，及时处理用户投诉，在收到投诉之日起7个工作日内与用户进行沟通，及时反馈投诉处理结果或最新进展。

③投诉办结。在与用户沟通一致后，申请机构应对投诉进行办结，并将投诉内容及处理情况存档备查。

如用户不满意申请机构给出的投诉处理结果，可进行自律投诉。

（2）自律投诉

1）投诉渠道

自律组织应建立健全创新应用的自律投诉机制，通过官方网站、微博、APP及申请机构营业网点等线上线下渠道，向公众公开长期有效的投诉电话、传真、电子邮箱、通信地址等。

2）投诉流程

投诉处理与处理流程主要包含以下流程：

①投诉受理。自律组织应及时受理公众投诉。

②投诉处理。自律组织应委派被投诉机构及时妥善处理投诉，并密切跟进投诉进展、处理投诉纠纷。被投诉机构应在收到投诉之日起7个工作日内与用户进行沟通，及时向自律组织反馈投诉处理结果和最新进展。

③组织调解。自律组织根据投诉情况进行调查分析，做出调解。如调解不成功，投诉人和被投诉机构可向相关测试管理部门反映和申诉。

④投诉办结。自律组织应在投诉处理完成后对投诉内容及处理情况存档备查。

（三）测试结束

1. 测试评价

（1）评估内容。从创新价值、服务质量、用户满意度、业务连续性保障、合法合规、交易安全、数据安全、风险防控（风控措施、补偿措施、应急处置、退出机制）等方面，评估创新应用是否严格履行声明书相关承诺、是否惠民利企、是否满足监管要求、是否商业可持续。

（2）评估方式

1）自测自评。测试机构应通过系统测试、内部审计等方式，组织开展内部评估工作，形成自评报告。

2）外部安全评估。测试机构可通过申请注册会计师审计等方式，对创新应用声明书相关承诺的落实情况进行评估，并获得证明材料。对于创新应用涉及的科技产品，测试机构可申请国家统一推行的金融科技技术产品通用安全认证，并获得证明材料。

3）第三方审计。对创新应用涉及的金融服务，测试机构可通过申请注册会计师审计等方式，对创新应用声明书相关承诺的落实情况进行评估，并获得证明材料。

4）专家论证。测试机构应组织相关领域外部权威专家组成专家组（至少包括业务、技术、安全、自律等专家），在自测自评基础上，结合外部评估情况进行综合评审论证。

2. 测试成功

（1）创新应用涉及的金融服务。相关管理细则①出台且通过专家论证、第三方审计的，报测试管理部门后，由出台管理细则的金融管理部门负责日常管理。

（2）创新应用涉及的科技产品。专家论证、外部评估均通过的，报测试管理部门后，可视情况在金融领域推广应用。通过专家论证但未通过外部评估的，报测试管理部门后，仅供联合申报测试的金融机构使用。

3. 测试退出

（1）退出流程

退出流程主要包含：

1）申请。申请机构应在停止服务前，至少提前15个工作日提出创新应用退出申请。

2）受理。自律组织从保护金融消费者合法权益、维护金融稳定等方面进行综合评估，并将评估结果报测试管理部门后反馈申请机构。

3）执行。申请机构应按照声明的退出方案执行退出程序。

---

① 金融管理部门结合测试运行情况按照现有职责分工，在条件具备前提下适时出台管理细则。

（2）退出方式

退出方式主要包含：

1）**主动退出。**申请机构出于战略定位、业务发展等方面考虑，拟终止创新应用运营服务的，可按退出流程主动申请退出。

2）**强制退出。**对未能严格落实本文件要求、未能履行声明书承诺且情节较为严重的创新应用，申请机构应按照要求执行退出流程，在保障金融消费者合法权益的前提下实现创新应用平稳退出。

3）**逾期退出。**对于测试运行 2 年以上仍未能通过测试评价的，申请机构应按流程退出测试。

五、发展愿景

（一）金融监管更加包容审慎

《中共中央 国务院关于新时代加快完善社会主义市场经济体制的意见》指出，要构建适应高质量发展要求的新型监管机制，健全对新业态的包容审慎监管制度。下一步，人民银行将认真落实党中央、国务院部署，切实履行国务院金融稳定发展委员会办公室职责，会同相关监管部门做好统筹与协同，强化监管顶层设计和整体布局，共同构建多层次、系统化的金融科技监管体系。**一是以创新监管工具为基础。**创新监管工具能够为金融科技创新提供一个底线清晰、适度宽松的发展环境，更好地适应金融科技风险复杂多变、产品日新月异等形势，为防范化解创新风险、增强金融监管效能提供基础支撑。**二是以监管规则为核心。**金融科技监管的关键是及时出台相应的监管规则，使创新有章可循、有规可依。通过创新监管工具，金融管理部门能够更好地掌握金融科技创新的服务模式、业务本质、风险机理等，加快出台监管规则，纾解因规则滞后带来的监管空白、监管套利等问题。**三是以数字化监管为手段。**监管规则的出台不是目的，重要的是抓好落地实施。创新监管工具将充分发挥数据、技术等生产要素作用，采用自然语言处理、知识图谱、深度学习等人工智能手段实现监管规则形式化、数字化和程序化，强化监管渗透的深度和广度，实现金融科技监管的数据加持、科技武装。在此基础上，包容审慎的金融科技监管体系基本建成，金融管理部门与创新主体、社会公众保持深度互动，共同构建起刚柔并济、更具弹性的创新试错、容错机制，在有效防范化解金融风险的同时，充分释放金融创新发展潜能。

（二）金融创新更加守正高效

创新是推动金融科技发展的不竭源泉，也是助推金融业转型升级的重要力量。在创新监管工具的示范带动作用下，市场主体将更加积极地运用科技手段破除金融发展瓶颈，创新金融产品、再造业务流程、提升服务质效，促进实体经济借助金融与科技"双翼"展翅翱翔。**金融机构**能够更好地拥抱科技、拥抱监管，精准把握市场脉搏，更好摸清用户最关心、最迫切的需求，从满足人民日益增长的美好生活需要出发，充分运用现代科技手段不断优化金融服务，提升金融服务精准性和可得性，使创新成果更具生命力。**科技公司**通过创新监管工具持续强化产用对接，与金融机构开展深度合作，更好地发挥在业务系统、算力存储、算法模型等方面的技术优势，紧密围绕金融创新的科技需求，在真实金融场景中加速核心技术攻关与研发，不断提升科技产品适配性、安全性和稳定性。

（三）金融服务更加惠民利企

在创新监管工具的引导下，金融机构更加专注于履行金融服务实体经济的初心使命，聚焦运用科技手段优化金融服务模式、丰富金融产品供给、扩大金融业务触达范围，打通普惠金融"最后一公里"，将金融业务无缝嵌入实体经济各领域，为市场主体和人民群众提供更便捷、更普惠的金融服务。**在金融惠民方面**，人民群众可通过创新监管工具，主动参与金融科技治理，积极从业务功能、信息保护、用户体验、风险补偿等方面对金融创新建言献策，助力金融服务满足不同客群个性化、多元化、差异化需求。**在金融利企方面**，创新监管工具将孵化出更多优质高效、安全便捷的金融创新，引导市场主体运用现代信息技术重构金融服务流程，释放数据生产要素价值，优化产业链供应链金融供给，将金融资源配置到经济社会发展的关键领域和薄弱环节，实现各类企业特别是民营小微企业金融服务的增量、扩面、提质、降本，为实体经济高质量发展注入金融活水。

（四）金融风控更加精准有效

安全是金融行业健康发展的根基，防范化解好科技应用风险对维护金融稳定、经济安全至关重要。创新监管工具运用新一代信息技术强化风险技防能力，加快对金融风险甄别、防范、化解新路径的探索，扎牢织密金融创新"安全网"。**一是**涵盖不同市场主体的风险事件报送机制、多方联动的风险监控平台基本建成，风险自动化、全天候的系统监测能力显著提升，及时准确掌握风险全局态势，实现**风险"看得见"。二是**监管知识图谱、风险数据仓库和智能化数字监管平台建设深入推进，运用人工智能、大数据等手段穿透业务多层嵌套、风险交叉传染等表象，准确把握金融风险的实质内容和关键所在，稳步提升风险特征刻画、关系分析、影响评估和趋势研判能力，做到**风险"辨得清"。三是**社会公众、创新主体、自律组织、政府部门间协同机制逐步完善，更加及时地向金融业和全社会发布风险提示预警，风险全面掌控能力和联合处置效率稳步提升，金融体系抵御风险能力全面提高，保障风险"管得住"。

1. Significance

1. 1   Building a new engine for financial transformation and upgrading

At present, a new round of global scientific and technological revolution and industrial transformation are developing vigorously, financial supply-side structural reform is being pushed forward, financial innovation and technology reform are evolving convergently, and digital transformation of finance have been a trend in industry development. The introduction of Innovation Regulatory Facility can accelerate the transition of financial regulatory pattern from passive supervision to active service, strengthen the leading, escorting and incubating role of regulation. It will guide financial institutions, technology companies and other market participants to better seize the historical opportunity of digital transformation, actively explore the application of new generation information technology to optimize product forms, service channels, business models and business processes, promote better application of technological innovation in the financial field, reduce the financial service costs, improve effectiveness, enhance digital transformation capabilities and core competitiveness, accelerate and empower the high-quality development of China's financial industry.

1.2 Addressing new challenges in the application of technology integration

With the continuous acceleration of the pace of digital technology renewal, technology and finance have been mutually integrated and successively iterated, and new products and business forms have emerged incessantly. In the early stage of financial innovation, as the business models are often not clear enough and the potential risks are not easy to identify, it is difficult to issue targeted regulatory rules and risk control measures in a timely manner. The Innovation Regulatory Facility introduces social supervision forces to create an inclusive and prudent innovation trial and error tolerance mechanism. This is conducive to releasing the vitality of technological innovation and discovering the potential of financial applications under the premise of complying with the law and protecting consumers' rights and interests. It is also conducive for financial regulatory authorities to deepen their understanding of the nature and risks of innovation in a scaled-down real market environment, accelerate the research and introduction of targeted regulatory rules, and effectively alleviate the regulatory challenges brought about by the development of digital finance.

1.3 Creating new facility for financial risk prevention and control

In the FinTech era, financial service channels are networked and digitalized, financial business is more virtual and boundaries are gradually blurred. Different businesses are interrelated and permeated each other, breaking the time and space limitations of traditional financial risk conduction. The speed and scale of risk propagation have increased exponentially, bringing new challenges to financial risk prevention and control. Innovation Regulatory Facility actively explores digitalized monitoring practice, constructs a multilevel, three-dimensional and comprehensive risk control system based on technical methods in order to realize multi-channel situation awareness, strengthen the joint prevention and control capability of cross-market, cross-industry and cross-regional financial risks, builds the "firewall" for new risks of FinTech innovations, and provides strong support for winning the battle to prevent and resolve financial risks.

1.4 Opening up new horizons in the regulation of financial innovation

Technology is neutral, with no distinction between good and bad. Proper application of technology can inject new impetus into financial development, while improper application may also trigger new risks. However, in order to cope with the impact on financial stability and financial market brought about by the integrated operation of institutions, cross-nesting of business and cross transmission of risks in the context of FinTech, some countries have adopted "one-size-fits-all" strict regulatory measures subjectively or objectively leading to the restriction of the technological innovation capacity of market participants and the failure to release their vitality. Innovation Regulatory Facility adopts the inclusive and prudent regulation concept with considering the innovation and security as an integrity, not only controls the risk of technology innovation application, but limit the impact of additional security measures in innovation efficiency. Innovation Regulatory Facility explores a new win-win model of FinTech regulation that requires both stability and development in practice, promote the synchronous development of innovation and safety, and focuses to enhance the professionalism, unity and penetration of financial regulation.

2. Regulatory Framework

2. 1　Guidelines

Firstly, **licensed operation**. The essence of FinTech is finance. Licensed operation of Financial business is the basic condition of testing application.　On the premise of meeting the general specifications, technology companies can directly apply for the testing and the involving financial service innovation and financial application scenarios should be provided by licensed financial institutions.　They can apply jointly with financial institutions or apply independently combined with the financial application scenarios to choose cooperative financial institutions.

Secondly, **legal compliance**. Security is an insurmountable bottom line and red line.　Financial institutions should comply with laws and regulations, manage and control the potential risks brought by new application of technology innovation, and ensure that innovation does not deviate from the correct direction.

Thirdly, **protection of rights and interests**.　Adhering to the people-centered development concept, we should establish and perfect a consumer rights protection mechanism suitable for the innovation and development of FinTech, with the practical protection for the legitimate rights and interests of financial consumers.

Fourthly, inclusiveness and prudence. We should practice the concept of flexible regulation, strengthen prudential regulation, and enhance regulatory inclusiveness to release the momentum of financial innovation and development.

2. 2 Design Rationale

"If a craftsman wants to do good work, he must first sharpen his tools. " (a quote from Confucius) The Innovation Regulatory Facility explores the establishment of a more penetrating and professional innovation regulation framework to improve the regulatory effectiveness of FinTech innovation. **Firstly, delineate a rigid bottom-line**. Based on current laws, regulations, departmental rules, and basic normative documents, we will clarify the red line for innovation with integrity in terms of business compliance, technical security, and risk control. **Secondly, set a flexible boundary**. To regulate in flexible ways, such as information disclosure and public supervision, supporting public to participate in FinTech governance and creating a moderately relaxed development environment for FinTech innovation. **Thirdly, reserve space for innovation**. Within the "rigid bottom-line", rational innovations are embraced, allowing market entities to enjoy equal opportunities and conditions to participate in innovation, making the best of modern information technology to improve the quality and efficiency of finance, and setting aside enough development space for truly valuable FinTech innovation.

2.3 Regulation Philosophy

Firstly, tackle the regulator's dilemma of " oversight or overplay", and make regulation more applicable. In the era of FinTech, financial services are more diversified, businesses boundaries become cross-nested, and risk control situations are more severe. Therefore, the traditional regulatory model has malfunctioned to some extent. Hence, on the premise of protecting the legitimate rights and interests of financial consumers, there is an urgent need for financial regulatory authorities to encourage financial industry institutions to innovate actively, and at the same time identify and avoid any defects and risks arose by innovation in a timely manner. The People's Bank of China create new Innovation Regulatory Facility. It aims to better balance safety and innovation. Aligned with China's flourishing FinTech innovation situation, Innovation Regulatory Facility explores a new way of FinTech regulation, which can not only guard the bottom line of safety, but also embrace rational innovation and be highly adapt to China's national conditions. This way of regulation should tackle the regulator's dilemma of " oversight or overplay ", standardize and guide the healthy and orderly development of FinTech.

Secondly, abandon the " one size fits all " simple model and enhance regulatory inclusiveness. From historical experience, proper regulation is the key to achieve effectiveness. Inadequate regulation can easily lead to a flood of fraudulent products pouring into the market, thus damaging the legitimate rights and interests of financial consumers; conversely, excessive regulation can easily lead to excessive compliance costs for financial industry institutions, thereby reducing innovation vitality. The intensity of regulation for Innovation Regulatory Facility is a key factor for regulatory authorities to consider. From the very beginning of the design, the People's Bank of China upholds the concept of tolerance, spontaneously abandons the "one size fits all" model, and actively explores new flexible regulatory approaches with increasingly guiding, inspiring and incentive features, and promotes information exchanges and benign interactions among government, innovation entities, and the public, forges a regulatory model consistent with the inherent development law of new things, and creates an inclusive FinTech innovation environment.

Thirdly, introduce a "multiple-linkage" public supervision mechanism to enhance the effectiveness of regulation. China has a large number of financial institutions, with financial service innovations in full swing, the traditional "government regulation + institutions autonomy" model is facing greater challenges. Introducing more external forces to participate in supervision is an effective means to optimize and innovate the regulation model. Considering that hundreds of millions of the public are the ultimate service targets of financial products, their opinions on the safety and convenience of innovative applications are paramount. To this end, the new

Innovative Regulatory Facility will introduce a public supervision mechanism to give full play to the role of different social subjects, help financial consumers get an in-depth understanding of the essence of innovative product functions, potential risks and compensation measures, so as to better protect their legitimate rights and interests. The Innovative Regulatory Facility will allow news media to play the role of a social radar to supervise the security, compliance and legitimacy of innovative products, and let third-party professionals participate in advance control and to comprehensively evaluate the reliability and effectiveness of the safety protection measures. Through the above-mentioned multiple-linkage supervision mechanism, a new mode of FinTech innovation regulation with "collaborative governance" will be promoted to enhance the effectiveness of regulation.

Fourthly, set up a "rigid threshold" for innovations and emphasize regulatory prudence. The development of FinTech cannot follow the old path of Internet finance. We must pay attention to both flexible regulation and prudential regulation. To some extent, financial innovation driven by science and technology is an exploration into unknown areas. Risks and variables follow each other closely. Improper response may exacerbate uncertainties and even cause systemic risks. To this end, the new Innovation Regulatory Facility emphasizes prudential regulation and strive to set a rigid threshold. From the perspective of finance, we insist that the essence of FinTech is finance. We should strictly implement the principles of financial licensed operation and prevent illegal and criminal activities such as illegal fund-raising and financial fraud by the name of "FinTech". From the perspective of science and technology, we should clarify the risk bottom line and safety standards, establish a risk control system for dynamic risk monitoring perception and efficient disposal, ensure that the truly valuable innovative technological achievements can be fully tested and iteratively improved, and finally inject technological impetus into financial innovation.

2.4 Governance system

Fully mobilize the enthusiasm of all parties in the society to create the "four in one" FinTech innovation governance system, which includes institutional autonomy, public supervision, industry self-discipline and government regulation.

Firstly, institutional autonomy. Financial institutions need to carry out the main responsibility for innovation management, strengthen internal risk control and self-discipline, actively accept public supervision and industry self-discipline, establish and perfect the mechanism of complaint response, emergency disposal, risk compensation and insurance indemnity, and effectively protect the legitimate rights and interests of users.

Secondly, public supervision. As the backbone of the governance system, the public can fully understand product information through multiple channels, recognize potential risks in time, and achieve full supervision of the "quality and effectiveness" of the FinTech innovation through suggestions, complaints, and appeals.

Thirdly , industry self-discipline. Industry associations play the role of a bridge in the governance system. They assist the government to handle complaints, publicize and implement training, and take self-discipline measures in a timely manner to provide strong support for the implementation of administrative requirements.

Fourthly , government regulation. As the leaders of the governance system, the financial regulatory authorities need to establish and improve the regulatory coordination and supervision implementation mechanism to ensure the implementation of various administrative measures.

3. Operation Mechanisms

3. 1　Security management mechanism

Financial security is an important part of national security. The development of FinTech should regard the protection of financial security as an insurmountable bottom line and red line. FinTech is a technology-driven financial innovation, the risks of which change dynamically and are highly unexpected and unpredictable. In order to better prevent and control innovation risks, ascertain the operation status of financial service testing and facilitate the timely issuance of targeted regulatory rules, Innovation Regulatory Facility adheres to the principle of inclusiveness and prudence, strictly abides by the bottom line of security, establishes and improve the security management mechanism covering the whole life-cycle of innovations before, during and after the event, and comprehensively builds a strong line of defense against the FinTech innovation risks.

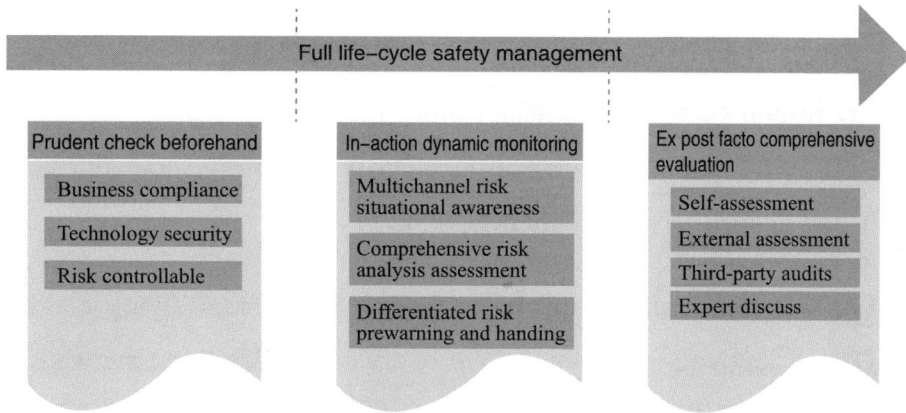

Full life–cycle safety management

Prudent check beforehand	In–action dynamic monitoring	Ex post facto comprehensive evaluation
Business compliance	Multichannel risk situational awareness	Self-assessment
Technology security	Comprehensive risk analysis assessment	External assessment
Risk controllable	Differentiated risk prewarning and handing	Third-party audits
		Expert discuss

Figure 1   Security management mechanism

3. 1. 1   Check carefully beforehand. First, taking business compliance as a premise, through internal institution audit, external professional assessment and consulting with management authorities, Innovation Regulatory Facility ensures that financial innovation does not cross the red line drew by laws and regulations, department regulations, and basic specification documents, and strictly prevents false innovation that breaks the existing business rules in the name of innovation. **Second, regarding technology safety as a guarantee**, Innovation Regulatory Facility prevents applications with technical vulnerabilities and potential risks from participating in the tests, by assessing against financial industry standards such as the General Specifications for Innovation Security, Personal Financial Information Protection Specifications, etc. , thus comprehensively improve the standard compliance and security of innovations, and ensure information technology is applied in the financial industry in a safe, reasonable and well-behaved manner. **Third, taking risk control as a key objective**, Innovation Regulatory Facility urges applicants to establish and perfect internal risk control systems, fulfill their responsibility of risk management, improve risk compensation, emergency response, service exit and other mechanisms, and practically protect user funds and information security, to firmly hold the bottom line against systemic financial risks.

3. 1. 2 Dynamically monitoring during the test. Relying on the FinTech innovation management service platform, Innovation Regulatory Facility uses digital regulation methods to continuously and dynamically monitor the operation status of innovations, and timely location, track, prevention and resolution of potential risks. **The first is the multi-channel risk situational awareness.** We strengthen cooperation with cyberspace administrations, public security departments, industry and information technology departments, establish synergy mechanism covering financial institutions, technology companies, industry associations, third-party professional institutions and government departments. We strengthen cooperation with regulatory authorities in cyberspace administration, public security, industry and information technology to achieve cross-industry, cross-department, and cross-field risk information sharing. We adopt methods such as institutional reporting, interface collection, and automatic detection to dynamically perceive the risk situation of FinTech applications based on artificial intelligence, big data and other technologies. **The second is comprehensive risk analysis and assessment.** We extract risk characteristic information, classify risks, and form a risk data warehouse. By using model analysis, expert review and other methods, we can accurately assess the scope of risk impact and the degree of harm. We analyze the relationship between different risk characteristics in depth, and timely detect risk trends and potential hidden dangers. **The third is differentiated risk early warning and disposal.** We establish a comprehensive prevention and control mechanism for innovation risks, and promote differentiated risk early warning and efficient emergency disposal. We guide testing institutions to fulfill their responsibilities for risk prevention and control, and with the help of third-party professional organization support capabilities, to consolidate the efforts of the financial industry and outsiders, to build a joint risk prevention and control mechanism, and to strictly achieve early detection of problems, early warning of risks, and early remediation of vulnerabilities. For risks and vulnerabilities that are difficult to remedy in a short term, we promptly release risk warnings and take comprehensive risk compensation measures; for innovations with major security issues, we can promptly block and expel them out of the test. If losses are incurred, the testing institution must compensate through risk provision funds, insurance plans, etc. , to practically protect the legitimate rights and interests of consumers.

3. 1. 3 Comprehensive evaluation afterwards. Innovation Regulatory Facility adopts methods such as self-test, self-evaluation, external evaluation, and expert review, to conduct comprehensive evaluation of innovations that are submitted to finalize the test, in terms of their innovation value, service quality, legal compliance, data security, risk prevention and control, etc. It includes whether the innovation fulfills the commitments in the statement, whether it benefits the people and enterprises, whether it meets regulatory requirements, and whether it is commercially sustainable, so as to identify and eliminate potential hazards in a timely manner, and prevent innovation risk spillovers. **The first is self-test and self-evaluation.** The applicant organizes internal evaluation through system testing and internal audit, and forms a self-evaluation report. **The second is external evaluation.** Through using the national uniformly promoted general safety certification for FinTech products, we conduct continuous dynamic security assessments of innovation-related technology products throughout their life cycle. **The third is the third-party audit.** By the CPA audit and other ways, evaluate the implementation of agreement related with innovation statement. **The fourth is expert review.** The application organizations organize external authoritative experts in related fields such as business, technology, security, self-discipline to form an expert group, based on self-test and self-evaluation results, to conduct comprehensive evaluation and review integrated external evaluation and the third-party audit.

3. 2　Innovation service mechanism

General Secretary Xi Jinping pointed out that innovation is the first driving force leading development. To implements the spirit of the CPC Central Committee and the State Council on building a service-oriented government, Innovation Regulatory Facility adheres to the concept of embedding regulation in service and promoting innovation through service, promotes the transformation of regulation mode from passive regulation to active service, actively builds innovative trial and error tolerance mechanisms and counseling optimization mechanisms. Innovation Regulatory Facility strengthens industry-user connection, government-enterprise coordination, and supply-demand matching, provides market entities with "all-round, three-dimensional and professional" regulatory service support, and create a fertile soil for the growth of FinTech innovation.

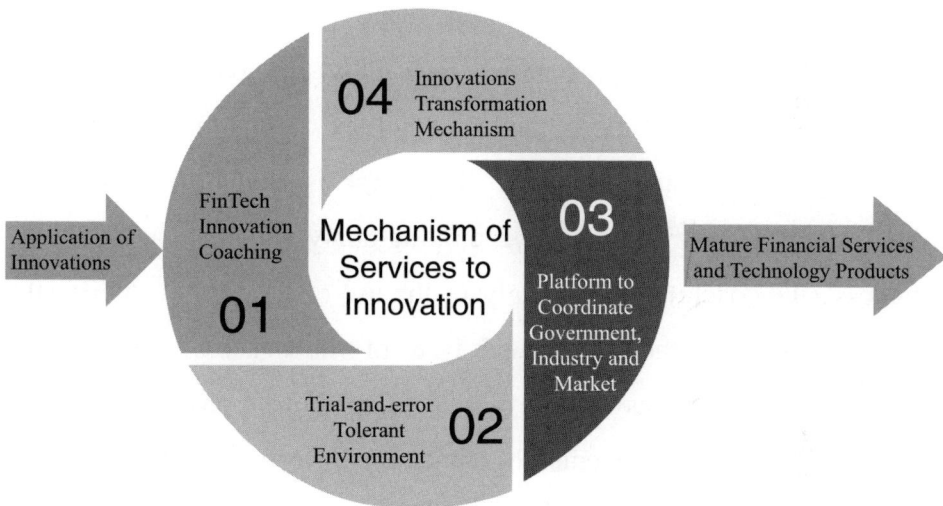

Figure 2   Innovation service mechanism

3. 2. 1   Carry out innovation coaching. The test administrative authorities organize and establish a professional coaching group to provide "one-on-one" professional regulatory guidance, so as to improve the safety and compliance of innovations and help them benefit the people and enterprises. Concerning application assistance, the coaching group maintains in-depth conversation with applicants, guiding them to continuously optimize the innovation in compliance, risk control, and consumer rights protection. For those with better foundation, the coaching group helps them improve the application materials; for those facing major problems, the coaching group supports them to change the topic. Although the application duration differs depending on the project itself status, eligible projects can eventually enter the test. In terms of business perspective, learning from the ideas of Business Process Model (BPM), Unified Modeling Language (UML) and other analysis tools, the coaching group assists applicants to accurately identify risk essence from the three dimensions of capital flow, data flow and partnership, and guide financial institutions and technology companies to better maintain integrity and innovate. **The first is the Capital Chain Analysis (CCA).** Through a penetrating analysis of the capital flow process, the coaching group analyzes the use of funds at each critical node, figures out the source and flow of funds across the chain, identify risks such as capital interception, misappropriation and idling, and strictly prevents the funds flow from real to false or illegal use, and to ensure financial services "transfuse blood and supply oxygen" for the real economy. **The second is Data Flow Analysis (DFA).** Through combing and characterizing the full life cycle of data, the coaching group tracks the flow and use of data between financial institutions, technology companies and consumers, defines the ownership, use rights, income rights, and management rights of data, and evaluates innovation applications in the data collection and use process on whether it is legal and compliant and fully authorized by users. For those involving the use of data by multiple parties, the working group should guide innovators to ensure data security through technology such as multi-party secure computing, tokenization and feature extraction. **The third is the Cooperative Relationship Analysis (CRA).** The coaching group uses the relationship map to sort out the division of responsibilities and powers among participant, coordinates with background investigations and core business logic analysis to ensure that FinTech innovation business backgrounds are real, business qualifications are valid and business models are sustainable.

3. 2. 2   Build a trial and error tolerance environment for innovations. Innovation is an exploratory practice, inevitably accompanied with risks and challenges. We should create an innovative atmosphere that "allowing trial and error, timely and rapid error correction" under the premise of maintaining stable finance and consumers' rights and interests. Innovation Regulatory Facility builds a test space with "error tolerance" capabilities. Under the strict prevention of innovation risk spillover, Innovation Regulatory Facility supports market participants to complete business chain practice and test for innovations' prototype of theory, technical model selection and business mode in real market environment, discover and remedy potential risks in time, effectively examines the innovation value, and creates high-quality product service rapidly, which meets not only the market demand but also regulatory requirements, through testing again and again, and full polish.

3. 2. 3   Build a connecting platform for government, industry, and users. Innovation Regulatory Facility gives full play to the advantages of "connecting one end to the market, one to the government, and one to users" in a miniaturized version of the real scenario, to deep activate the elements and resources of innovations, and to promote development of FinTech innovations. **In terms of industry and market connecting**, through experience communication, practices sharing, joint research, industry cooperation, etc., we strengthen the connection and collaboration between financial institutions and technology companies, achieve efficient matching between financial institutions' application needs and technology companies' supply, and enhance the transformation of technological innovations to financial applications. **In terms of government-enterprise collaboration**, financial regulatory authorities and market entities continuously strengthen beneficial interactions through symposiums, coaching, window guidance, etc., gradually clarify the goals of innovation and development directions during the interaction, and guide the upright and innovation of FinTech. **In terms of matching supply and demand**, through measures such as information disclosure, complaint and supervision, the communication channels between the supply and demand parties are unblocked, so that financial consumers can better understand the essence of innovative application functions, suggest and express the core appeals, and innovative participants can know the needs of consumers and develop hard core products. As a result, the direct and deep communication between production, study, scientific research and practical are strengthened, and a mutual promotion and smooth connection between produce and application is formed, which injects new energy into high-quality development in finance.

3. 2. 4   Improve the mechanism of innovation achievements transformation. The first is to strengthen the vitality of innovation achievement through the standardization. We organize and establish a special standard working group, continuously summarize the experience of testing and operation, guide testing institutions to build and perfect the standard system of enterprise, and actively join in making industry and national standard. By means of standardization, we should manage the safety gate, fasten the application scale, and fasten the compliance criterion well. Meanwhile, there should be a high standard for ensuring high quality, gathering the elements of knowledge, technology, talent, data, etc. , in order to realize the transformation of old and new kinetic energy of enterprise development, gradually build the strength of quality and brand, and increasingly promote the vitality of FinTech innovative achievement. **The second is to strengthen the impact of innovative achievement by building exhibition platform.** The excellent innovative achievements, which are controllable risk, benefiting people and enterprises, should be summarized regularly or irregularly. The industry associations, alliances and joint laboratories are used to refine the best innovative experiences, improve the demonstration and influence of innovative achievement, and accelerate the transformation and landing of excellent achievements, through the methods of compiling and distributing excellent practices database, holding exhibition forum, issuing product evaluation report, etc. **The third is to lower the transmission costs of innovative achievement by strengthening**

policy support. We should make use of the "two hands" of government and market, fully give play to the guiding role of the government with the decisive role of the market in allocating resources, at the same time we should strengthen the policy and capital support for excellent innovation projects, broaden enterprise financing channel, scatter technical innovation costs, motivate internal development vitality of market participants, and jointly build effective ecology of FinTech industry development.

3.3 Information disclosure mechanism

Information disclosure is an effective means to protect the legitimate rights and interests of financial consumers and strengthen the self-discipline of financial market entities. Innovation Regulatory Facility, established in accordance with the spirit of the CPC Central Committee and the State Council on deepening the reform of "decentralized governance, flexible regulation and optimized services", draws on new measures such as the notification and commitment system, comprehensively employs declaration, management registration, user explicit declarations and multiple measures to establish a mechanism for proactive information disclosure, overall transparency and proactive commitment that covers the entire life cycle of innovations, simplifies the testing and application process, releases the innovation vitality of market entities, improve the timeliness, transparency and credibility of information disclosure, so as to provide strong support on FinTech innovation risks prevention and innovation regulation efficiency improvement.

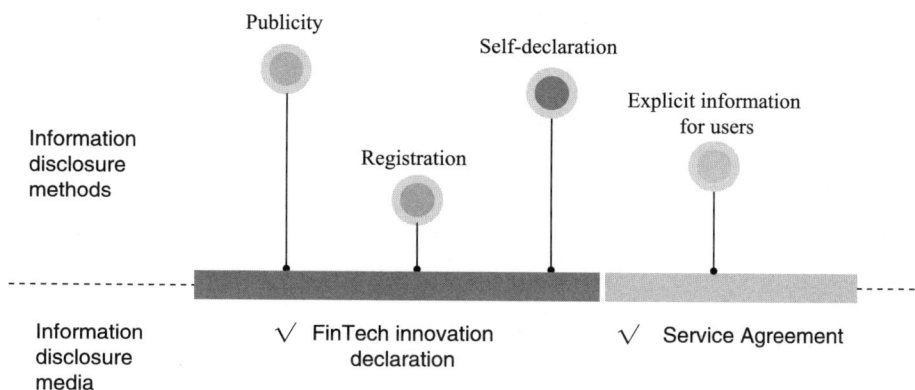

Publicity

Self-declaration

Explicit information
for users

Information
disclosure
methods

Registration

Information
disclosure
media

√ FinTech innovation
declaration

√ Service Agreement

Figure 3   Information disclosure mechanism

3. 3. 1   Information disclosure media. The first is the statement.

As the medium of information disclosure methods such as publicity,
registration, and self-declaration, the statement mainly includes
elements such as basic information, service information, innovation
descriptions, evaluation reports, risk prevent and control measures,
and complaint response. **The second is service agreement.** As a
carrier of explicit information for users, the service agreement
mainly contains information such as innovative application functions
and services, responsibilities and rights, risk compensation, and
data authorization. Financial consumers can fully understand the
Functional substance of innovative services through the service
agreement, and use financial services on the premise of being fully
informed, thus consumer disputes caused by information asymmetry
can be effectively prevented.

3. 3. 2   Information disclosure methods. The first is publicity.

Disclosure of innovation element information to the public through
the statement, so that the people can understand the real status of

innovation in a timely manner, identify potential risks and make suggestions for improvement. **The second is registration**. The applicant shall register the information of innovative application with the test administrative authority as required, so that the test administrative authority can grasp the actual status of innovations, effectively assess potential risks, and issue targeted regulatory rules faster. **The third is self-declaration**. Applicants make self-declarations on innovations through online and offline channels such as official websites and physical outlets, and make promises to the public on the authenticity, accuracy and completeness of the self-declared content, to strengthen the self-monitoring awareness of innovation institutions, and boost consumer confidence. **The fourth is explicit information for users**. Before users use financial services, the innovation institution clearly notifies users about the relevant elements of innovative applications through the service agreement. On this basis, based on the FinTech innovation management service platform, we establish an information disclosure mechanism covering the entire life cycle of the innovation to enable that all relevant parties can timely and accurately grasp the latest status of the innovative application.

3.4 Rights protection mechanism

Financial consumers are the ultimate service target of financial services. Regulating the behavior of innovative entities, and maintaining a fair and just market environment are important goals for the supervision of FinTech innovation. A reasonable and effective rights protection mechanism helps to enhance financial consumers' confidence in the finance market, and enhance their willingness to use innovative services and participate in innovative designs. Innovation Regulatory Facility, through a package of measures such as building a platform for announcements and improving risk compensation mechanisms, takes multiple measures to guide and regulate the behavior of innovative entities, protect the legitimate rights and interests of consumers, and promotes the healthy and sustainable development of financial technology innovation.

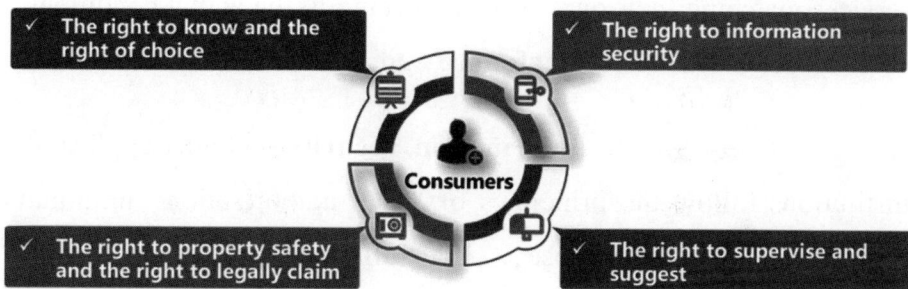

Figure 4   Rights protection mechanisms

3. 4. 1   The right to know and the right of choice. The first is easy to obtain the information. Through the official website of the application institution, microblog, APP, and physical outlets, with various methods such as publicity, self-declaration, and explicit information for users, Innovation Regulatory Facility provides sufficient information access channels to enhance the disclosure information Availability. **The second is true and comprehensive content.** The Innovation Regulatory Facility fully discloses the content and information of the functional services, potential risks, preset compensation measures, complaint response mechanisms and other aspects of FinTech innovation, and re-publicizes changes in important information to improve the authenticity and completeness of the content of innovation declaration. **The third is easy to understand the language.** Supervise application institution uses simple and clear language to provide necessary introductions and explanations on professional terms and industry background, so that financial consumers can understand the declaration easily. Through the above measures, financial consumers can have a comprehensive understanding of innovative applications, and can choose financial services matching their own needs according to the actual conditions, so as to better ensure their informed and independent choices.

3.4.2 The right to information security. Guide application institutions follow the principles of "user authorization, minimum sufficient, special purpose, and full protection", We will strengthen life-cycle security management of data and establish and improve long-term prevention and control mechanisms for information security, fully assess potential risks, control information security thresholds, and strictly prevent data leakage, tampering, damage and improper use. **When data is being collected**, the purpose, method, and scope of user data collection and use should be clearly stated through authorization agreements, etc., and data can be collected after obtaining user authorization. **When data is stored**, it is required to take full use of measures comprehensively such as encrypted storage, access control, tokenization and security audits to enhance data security and privacy protection capabilities and reduce the risk of data leakage. **When data is being used**, the application mechanism of data trust sharing and fusion is established and it is required to provide only desensitized calculation results under the premise of not collecting or sharing the original data and promote better data empowerment of innovation. **when services are withdrawn**, data cleaning and privacy protection should be done in accordance with relevant national and financial industry regulations.

3. 4. 3 The right to property safety and the right to claim under the law. The safety of property funds is related to the vital interests of financial consumers. We should not only be prepared to fight against and fend off risks, but also take measures in advance to avert danger and turn the corner, so as to provide "double insurance" for financial innovation to ensure property safety. **In terms of property safety**, it is necessary to urge applicant institutions to enrich risk prevention measures, implement relevant requirements of the state and financial administration, improve the safety management mechanism of fund raising, use and return, and adopt strict internal control and monitor methods to ensure the safety of consumer property and funds, make sure take precautions and be prepared before risks occur. In terms of seeking compensation under the law, it is required to clarify the identification method of risk responsibility, set up fast payment channels for consumers, and support risk provision funds, insurance plans and other compensation measures to effectively protect the legitimate rights and interests of consumers. For financial losses that are not caused by the customers' own responsibility, it is required to provide full compensation to effectively protect the consumer's property from loss, and to make sure losses retrievable.

3.4.4 **The right to supervise and suggest.** Establish a multi-level complaint and suggestion mechanism, unblock complaints and suggestions acceptance channels, and more effectively resolve disputes. **The first is to do a good job of institutional complaints.** As the main body responsible for handling complaints and suggestions, the application institution publicizes the acceptance method and handling mechanism to the public through prominent locations in outlets, official websites, mobile applications and other channels. Application institutions shall deal with and give feedback to public complaints and suggestions within the specified time limit. **The second is to pay attention to self-discipline and complaints.** Self-regulatory organizations establish and improve the self-regulatory complaint mechanism, closely follow up the progress of complaint handling by the complained institution, and organize mediation as needed. **The third is to implement government supervision.** If the self-regulatory organization fails the mediation, financial consumers can appeal to the test administration authority. The test administration authority conducts investigations, verification and feedback in a timely manner to effectively protect the legitimate rights and interests of consumers.

4. Implementation protocols

Without rules, nothing can be done, FinTech innovation can't be separated from the escort of effective rules and regulations. The People's Bank of China has analyzed in depth the nature and objective rules of the risks of financial applications of new technologies, studied and formulated rules and norms that are not only conducive to the innovation and development of financial technology, but also meet the needs of financial governance, and gradually established a basic rule system for the FinTech regulation that is comprehensive, complete, rigorous and mutually supportive. Rely on the certification system implemented by the state to promote the implementation of rules and regulations, and strive to improve the ability with integrity of FinTech innovation and comprehensive governance level. Among others, **Testing specification for FinTech innovation (JR/T 0198 – 2020)** is the basic rule for the management of FinTech innovation. It regulates the whole life cycle of innovation testing from the implementation level, and specifies the requirements on declaration format, testing process, risk control mechanism, evaluation mode, etc. , providing common guidelines for financial administrations, self-regulatory organizations, financial institutions and technology companies to carry out finTech innovation practices.

The details of the specification are as follows.

4.1 Test declaration

4.1.1 Declaration requirements

True and accurate: The declaration shall be true, accurate, complete, and timely. It is not allowed to make false records, misleading statements, omit or delay the publicity of innovative application information.

Concision and clarity: The declaration shall use simple and easy to understand language, provide necessary introduction and explanation of the professional terminology and background, industry knowledge, etc., so that users can conveniently understand the information of innovation.

Consistency of information: The declaration shall be in Chinese. If a foreign language version is used at the same time, the content of each text should be consistent. If there is any ambiguity between the texts, Chinese text shall prevail.

Legal compliance: The declaration shall comply with the relevant provisions of laws and regulations on state secrets, commercial secrets, personal information protection, and intellectual property protection.

Long-term preservation: The declaration materials shall be properly retained for at least 20 years from the date of publication.

Completeness of declaration: The applicant has not regulated, but may lead to significant misunderstanding and wrong judgment of users, due to undeclared relevant information. In this situation, application institution should declare such information promptly.

4.1.2 Forms of declaration

(1) Publicity

Publicity time and channel: The application institution shall apply for publicity at least 25 working days before the innovation is officially provided as a service to the users. The publicity period shall be 5 working days. When FinTech innovation application changes significantly during the publicity period, the application institution shall update the information in time and reapply for publicity.

Form of publicity: It should be publicized in the form of FinTech innovation declaration. The statement should include basic information of innovative application, service information, legal compliance assessment, technological safety assessment, risk prevention and control, complaint response mechanism, commitment statement and other elements, see 4.1.3 Declaration elements for further details.

(2) Registration

Registration time and channel: The application institution shall apply for registration within 5 working days after the innovation application is publicized.

Form of registration: The applicant institution shall register in the form of FinTech innovation declaration.

(3) Self-declaration

Self-declaration time and channel: The application institution shall make self-declarations at a prominent position on its official website, microblog page, in its APPs, branches and other online and offline channels, after completing the registration and before officially providing services to the users. The application institution shall make a commitment to the public for the authenticity, accuracy and completeness of the self-declaration.

Form of self-declaration: The application institution shall be self-declared in the form of Fintech innovation declaration.

(4) Explicit information for users

Time and channel of explicit information for users: The application institution shall clearly inform the user the elements which need to be explicit information in statement when the user signs the contract.

Forms of explicit information for users: The applicant institution shall come to the explicit information for users in the form of service agreement, and provide users with channels for inquiry and download.

4.1.3 Declaration elements

(1) Basic information of innovation application

Innovation application identifier: The innovation identifier should consist of 26 digits of letters and numbers, which is made up by three parts: the application institution's unified social credit identifier (18 digits), as shown on its business license; the year innovation declaration is submitted (4 digits); and the project number (4 digits). The dash ("-") is used to separate the parts. This applies to public publicity, registration, self-declaration and explicit information for users (see table 1).

Example: Application institution A has a unified social credit identifier of 91210200TK0QE7GT5L, then the identifier of its fifth innovation declaration in year 2019 should be 91210200TK0QE7GT5L - 2019 - 0005.

Table 1 Composition of the Innovation Identifier

Part 1	Part 2	Part 3
unified social credit identifier (18 digits)	year innovation declaration was submitted (Arabic number, 4 digits)	project number (Arabic number, 4 digits, starting from 0001)

Innovation name: Innovation name should be concise, clear and easy to understand, and should not exceed 20 words in principle. It is applicable to publicity, registration, self-declaration and explicit information for users.

Innovation type: Innovation type include financial services and technological products. It is applicable to publicity, registration, self-declaration and explicit information for users.

Institutional information

Unified social credit identifier: Unified social credit code on the business license of the application institution should be filled in. It is applicable to publicity, registration, self-declaration and explicit information for users.

Legal entity identifier: Legal entity identifier of the application institution should be filled in, if any. It is applicable to publicity, registration, self-declaration and explicit information for users. If not any, do not fill in.

Institution name: The application institution's name as shown on its business license should be filled in. It is applicable to public announcement, registration, self-declaration and explicit information for users.

Financial license information: The financial license information of the licensed financial institutions participating in the innovation should be filled in includes the name of the license, the issuing authority and the license number. It is applicable to publicity, registration, self-declaration and explicit information for users. If not any, do not fill in.

Proposed date of operation: The time when the innovative application intends to provide services to users should be filled in the format is yyyy/mm/dd, for example: 2019/02/27. It is applicable to publicity, registration and self-declaration.

Technologies applied: In principle, no more than 150 words should be used to briefly describe the modern information technology used and its functions for financial services. It is applicable to publicity, registration and self-declaration.

Functional services: It should describe the main service and function information provided by innovative application for users, and indicate whether there are any third-party organizations involved in the R&D and operation and maintenance process, and clarify their participation links and work contents. In principle, it should not exceed 200 words. It is applicable to publicity, registration and self-declaration.

Explanation of innovativeness: It is necessary to describe the innovative points of the project in technology application or financial service, and clarify the innovation of innovations. It is applicable to publicity, registration, self-declaration and explicit information for users.

Expected result: In principle, no more than 50 words should be used to briefly describe the expected social benefits and market value of the innovative application after it goes online. It is applicable to publicity, registration, self-declaration and explicit information for users.

Expected scale: In principle, no more than 50 words should be used to briefly describe the expected scale of the innovative application after it goes online. Expected scale includes but is not limited to the number of users, transaction volume, transaction volume and other quantitative indicators. It is applicable to publicity, registration, self-declaration and explicit information for users.

(2) Innovation application service information

Service channel: It should describe the channels or channels of innovative application provided by the application institution to users. It is applicable to publicity, registration, self-declaration and explicit information for users.

Service time: It should describe the time frame that innovative application can complete the service normally. It is applicable to publicity, registration, self-declaration and explicit information for users.

Service user: It should describe the applicable population for innovative applications. It is applicable to publicity, registration, self-declaration and explicit information for users.

Service agreement: It should fill in the relevant contents that users need to know and agree when using this innovation application. It is applicable to publicity, registration and self-declaration.

(3) Legal compliance assessment

Assessment institution: It should fill in full Chinese name of assessment institution. It is applicable to publicity, registration, self-declaration and explicit information for users.

Assessment date: It should fill in the time when the assessment agency issues the legal compliance assessment materials. The format is yyyy/mm/dd, for example, 2019/02/27. It is applicable to publicity, registration, self-declaration and explicit information for users.

Term of validity: It should fill in the validity period of legal compliance evaluation materials. The format is x year (s), for example: 3 years. It is applicable to publicity, registration, self-declaration and explicit information for users.

Assessment conclusion: In principle, no more than 100 words should be used to briefly describe the conclusion of legal compliance assessment. It is applicable to publicity, registration, self-declaration and explicit information for users.

Assessment materials: It should provide legal compliance assessment materials for innovative applications. Assessment materials include but not limited to assessment basis, assessment method, assessment analysis and assessment conclusion. It is applicable to publicity, registration and self-declaration.

(4) Technological security assessment

Assessment institution: It should fill in full Chinese name of assessment institution. It is applicable to publicity, registration, self-declaration and explicit information for users.

Assessment date： It should fill in the time when the assessment agency issues the legal compliance assessment materials. The format is yyyy/mm/dd, for example, 2019/02/27. It is applicable to publicity, registration, self-declaration and explicit information for users.

Term of validity： It should fill in the validity period of legal compliance evaluation materials. The format is x year, for example： 3 years. It is applicable to publicity, registration, self-declaration and explicit information for users.

Assessment conclusion： In principle, no more than 100 words should be used to briefly describe the conclusion of technology security assessment. It is applicable to publicity, registration, self-declaration and explicit information for users.

Assessment materials： It should provide legal compliance assess-ment materials for technology security. Assessment materials include but not limited to assessment basis, assessment method, assessment analysis and assessment conclusion. It is applicable to publicity, registration, self-declaration and explicit information for users.

(5) Risk prevention and control

Risk prevention and control measures： It should describe potential risks that an innovative application may pose to the security of the user's capital or sensitive information, and describe the protection taken to address them. It is applicable to publicity, registration, self-declaration and explicit information for users.

Risk compensation mechanism: It should describe the potential risks that may exist in the innovative application and describe the precautions taken against them. It is applicable to publicity, registration, self-declaration and explicit information for users.

Exit mechanism: It should describe the exit mechanism from innovation testing for innovation applications. The exit mechanism shall be able to ensure data security, prevent the risk of fund theft, and achieve smooth exit when the innovation application exits normally or when it exits abnormally due to special circumstances. The exit mechanism includes but is not limit to withdrawal conditions, withdrawal plan, execution department, capital flow. It is applicable to public announcement, registration and self-declaration.

Emergency plan: It should submit emergency plans for innovation applications. Emergency plans shall be useful in improving the application institution's comprehensive management and emergency response capability in case of emergencies. The emergency plan includes but is not limit to definition and classification of emergencies, handling principles, prevention and early warning mechanisms, emergency support, emergency training and drills. It is applicable to public announcement, registration and self-declaration.

(6) Complaint response mechanism

Institutional complaints

Complaint channels: It should fill in channel information of receiving user complaints. Channel information includes but not limit to branch addresses, mailing addresses, telephone numbers, fax numbers, email addresses, official websites, microblog accounts, and APPs. It is applicable to publicity, registration, self-declaration and explicit information for users.

Complaint acceptance and handling mechanism: It should fill in relevant contents of complaint acceptance and handling mechanism. Relevant contents include but not limited to accepted department, accepted time, handling procedures, and handling time limit. It is applicable to publicity, registration, self-declaration and explicit information for users.

Self-discipline complaint

Complaint channels: It should fill in the channel information of receiving self-discipline complaints. The channel information includes but not limited to branch addresses, mailing addresses, telephone numbers, fax numbers, email address, official website, microblog accounts, and APPs. It is applicable to publicity, registration, self-declaration and explicit information for users.

Complaint acceptance and handling mechanism: It should fill in the relevant contents of self-discipline complaint acceptance and handling mechanism according to the requirements of industry self-discipline. The relevant contents include but not limited to acceptance department, acceptance time, handling procedures, and handling time limit. It is applicable to publicity, registration, self-declaration and explicit information for users.

(7) Commitment statement

The application institution shall make a commitment statement on FinTech innovation declaration's authenticity, accuracy and completeness, with the institution's official seal.

4. 1. 4 Declaration process

The declaration mainly consists of the following processes:

(a) **Preparation**. The application institution shall strictly comply with existing laws, regulations, departmental rules and normative documents, establish and improve internal control, security control, emergency disposal, service withdrawal and other mechanisms in accordance with the **Security general specification for FinTech innovation** (JR/T 0199 – 2020). It shall adopt risk provision funds, insurance plans and other measures to maximize compensation for the user losses caused by risk events, and effectively protect the legitimate rights and interests of financial consumers. When a technology company acts as the application institution, the technology products must have a corresponding financial scenario provided by a licensed financial institution.

(b) **Application**. The application institution should fill in the FinTech innovation declaration as required, and submit application through the management service platform for FinTech innovation.

(c) **Acceptance**. The test management departments and the self-regulatory organizations[①] verify that the declaration submitted by the application institution are well-formed, complete, consumer-fair, and reasonable in content. If verified, the self-regulatory organizations should assess the potential impact of the innovation, and the assessment reports shall be submitted to the financial management departments in charge of the test (referred to as the test management departments). If verification fails, the process goes back to Step (a).

(d) **Public announcement**. The test management departments and self-regulatory organizations should publicity the declaration on the fintech innovation management service platform.

(e) **Supervision**. During publicity, the application institution shall accept public supervision on the legality, compliance and rationality of the statement. If the public have any opinion on its content, they can report to the self-regulatory organizations, according to Step (f); If there is no opinion, publicity is considered approved, and the process goes to (g).

(f) **Opinion processing**. The self-regulatory organization shall sum-

---

① The self-regulatory organization is delegated by the testing administrative department to carry out relevant self-regulatory work such as the review and publicity of the FinTech innovation test statement.

marize and feedback public opinions to the application institution in a timely manner. After feedback received, the application institution shall properly communicate with the opinion owner to reach an a-greement, and report the handling of public opinions result to the self-regulatory organization within 5 working days.

(g) **Assessment**. The self-regulatory organization shall analyze and assess the opinion handling, and report relevant situations to the test management departments for verification and confirmation. If the assessment fails, return to Step (a).

(h) **Registration**. After the assessment's approval, the application institution shall register as required. For related technology products, a certificate of compliance with the JR/T 0199 – 2020 standard issued by an external authority shall be submitted before registration.

(i) **Self-declaration**. After registration, the application institution shall make a self-declaration in accordance with this document.

(j) **Explicit information for users**. The application institution shall collect user agreement consent in accordance with this document when the user signs a contract.

(k) **Modification**. In case of any modification in the key elements of the declaration, the application institution shall refill the declaration and redo the whole declaration process according to the procedures.

4. 2   Test operation

4. 2. 1   Internal risk control

The application institutions should establish and improve internal risk control systems, properly assign risk management responsibilities, regularly carry out innovation security audits and assessments, clarify the management responsibilities of various positions and personnel, improve the emergency response and accountability mechanisms for risk events. Third-party organizations that participate in innovative application design and development, security assessment shall strictly abide by the relevant national and financial industry management requirements and ensure no risk management responsibility transfer.

4. 2. 2   Risk monitoring

Self-regulatory organizations shall use the management service platform for FinTech innovation to continuously and dynamically monitor the operation status of innovations application in accordance with **Risk monitoring specification for FinTech product innovation** (JR/T 0200 – 2020), strengthen external risk perception, timely locate, track, prevent and resolve potential risks in its testing operations, and regularly report to the test management departments. The application institutions shall promptly report important events, operation records and system logs to the self-regulatory organization during the innovation test period.

4. 2. 3 Risk handling

The application institution shall establish and improve a comprehensive risk treatment and compensation mechanism, promote differentiated risk warning and efficient emergency response, ensure early detection of problems, early exposure of risks, and early treatment of vulnerabilities. For risks and vulnerabilities that are difficult to remedy in the short term, comprehensive risk compensation measures should be promptly taken. For innovations that have severe security risks or that have undergone major risk events, relevant information should be promptly reported to the test management agencies and self-regulatory organizations, and the test shall be withdrawn as appropriate. In case of financial losses, compensations should be made through risk provision funds, insurance plans, etc. , to effectively protect the rights and interests of consumers.

4. 2. 4 Complaints and suggestions

(1) Institution complaints

Complaint channels: The application institution shall establish a complaint mechanism. The application institution shall disclose the long-term effective complaint telephone number, fax, e-mail address and correspondence address to the public through official website, micro-blog, app, business outlets and other prominent online and offline channels.

Complaint process

The main processes for receiving and handling complaints are as follows:

(a) **Complaint acceptance:** The application institution shall promptly accept user's complaints.

(b) **Complaint handling:** The application institution shall fully understand the complaint situation, handle user complaints in a timely manner, communicate with user within 7 working days from the date of acceptance of the complaint, and provide timely feedback on the results or latest update.

(c) **Handling of complaints:** The application institution shall settle the complaint and archive the content and handling process of the complaint for future reference after communicating with the user and reaching an agreement.

If user is not satisfied with the complaint handling result that given by the application institution, the user can make a self-regulatory complaint.

(2) **Self-regulatory complaints**
Complaint channels: The Self-regulatory organizations shall establish and improve a self-regulatory the complaint mechanism for innovations, and make information available to the public through its official website, microblog page, APP, branches, and other online and offline channels, all in a prominent position. Information disclose should include long-term and effective complaint hotline numbers, fax numbers, email addresses, and mailing addresses.

Complaint process

The main processes for receiving and handling complaints are as follows:

(a) **Complaint acceptance:** The Self-regulatory organizations shall promptly accept public complaints.

(b) **Complaint handling:** The self-regulatory organization shall delegate to the complained institution the prompt and proper handling of the complaint, follow up the progress closely, and handle any dispute. The complained institution shall communicate with user within 7 working days from the date of the acceptance complaint, feedback the results and latest update to the self-regulatory organization in a timely manner.

(c) **Organizing mediation:** The self-regulatory organization investigates and analyzes the complaint and mediate both parties. If the mediation is unsuccessful, the complainant and the complained institution can report and appeal to the relevant test management institution.

(d) **Complaint settlement:** The self-regulatory organization shall archive the content and handling process of the complaint for future reference after the complaint is handled.

4. 3 Test closure

(1) Test assessment

Assessment content: Assessment content includes innovation value, service quality, customer satisfaction, business continuity guarantee, legal compliance, transaction security, data security, risk prevention and control (risk control measures, compensation measures, emergency disposal, exit mechanism), etc. to assess whether the innovation strictly fulfills the relevant commitments in the declaration, whether it benefits individuals and enterprises, whether it meets the regulatory requirements, and whether the business model is sustainable.

Assessment method: Self-test and self-assessment, external assessment, expert assessment.

Self-test and self-assessment: The testing institution shall carry out internal evaluation and form self-evaluation report by system testing and internal audit, etc.

External security assessment: The testing institutions can assess the implementation of the commitments related to the declaration of innovative application and obtain supporting documentation, for example, by applying for a CPA audit. For technology products involved in the innovation, the testing institutions can apply for the universal safety certification of FinTech products promoted by the state, and obtain certification materials.

Third-party audits: For financial services involved in innovative applications, testing institutions can assess the implementation of commitments related to the statement of innovative application, for example, applying for audits by certified public accountants, etc. , and obtain certification materials.

Expert assessment: The testing institutions shall organize external authoritative experts in related fields to form an expert group (including at least experts from the relevant business, technology, security, and self-regulation areas), conduct comprehensive assessment with the situation of external evaluation based on previous self-assessment and external assessment results.

(2) Test success
Financial services involved in innovative applications: If relevant management rules① are issued and the test assessment passed expert assessment, third-party audit, after report to the test management departments, the financial management department, which issues the management rules, manages the routine. If conditions are met, the financial management departments shall issue the management rules based on current division of responsibilities and the test outcome.

Technology products involved in innovation applications: If the expert assessment and external assessment are passed, after report to the test management departments, the technology products can ex-

---

① The financial regulatory authorities shall issue the regulatory rules based on current division of responsibilities and the test outcome.

tend its application in financial sector as appropriate. Those that have passed the expert assessment but failed the external assessment can only be used by financial institutions that have jointly applied for the test after reporting to the test management departments.

(3) Test exit

Exit process

The exit process mainly consists of the following processes:

(a) **Application**: The application institution shall submit an innovation withdrawal application at least 15 working days in advance before service termination.

(b) **Acceptance**: The self-regulatory organizations shall conduct comprehensive evaluations in terms of legitimate rights and interests and maintain financial stability, report the evaluation results to the testing management department and then update the application institution.

(c) **Execution**: The application institution shall execute exit process in accordance with the declared exit plan.

Exit method

There are three methods to exit:

(a) **Voluntary exit**: Application institutions which intend to terminate the innovation services due to strategic or business development considerations can actively apply for withdrawal according to the withdrawal process.

(b) **Forced exit**: For innovations that fail to implement the require-ments of this document, fail to fulfill the commitments in the state-ment, or have more severe circumstances, the application institution shall execute the exit process as required, and withdraw the innova-tion services smoothly under the premise of protecting the legitimate rights and interests of financial consumers.

(c) **Application expire exit**. The application institution shall with-draw according to the procedure for not passing the test assessment in 2 years since the test starts.

5. Development Vision

5. 1   Financial regulation being more inclusive and prudent

The Opinions of the Central Committee of the Communist Party of China and the State Council on Accelerating the Improvement of the Socialist Market Economic System in the New Era pointed out that it is necessary to build a new type of regulatory mechanism that meets the requirements of high-quality development, and improve an inclusive and prudent regulatory system for new businesses. In the next step, the People's Bank of China will conscientiously implement the arrangements of the CPC Central Committee and the State Council, practically fulfill the responsibilities of the Office of the State Council's Financial Stability and Development Commission, coordinate with relevant regulatory authorities, strengthen the top-level design and overall layout of supervision, and jointly build a multi-level and systematic FinTech regulatory system. **The first is to be based on Innovation Regulatory Facility**. Innovation Regulatory Facility can provide a moderately flexible development environment with clear lines for FinTech innovation, better adapt to the complex and changeable FinTech risks, rapid product changes and other complicated situations, and provide basic support for preventing and defusing innovation risks and enhancing financial regulatory effectiveness. **The second is to focus on regulatory rules**. The key to FinTech regulation is to promptly promulgate relevant rules and regulations for innovation to follow. Through Innovation Regulatory Facility, financial administration departments can better grasp the service model, business nature, and risk mechanism of FinTech innovation, speed up the introduction of regulatory rules, and alleviate regulatory gaps and arbitrage problems caused by regulatory lag. **The third is to employ digital supervision**. The promulgation of regulatory rules is not the destination, but the important thing is to implement them. Innovation Regulatory Facility will give full play to the role of data, technology and other production factors, and adopt natural language processing, knowledge graphs, deep learning and other artificial intelligence methods to achieve formalization, digitization and proceduralization of regulatory rules, strengthen the depth and breadth of regulatory penetration, and realize a data and technology armed FinTech regulatory system. On this basis, an inclusive and prudent FinTech supervision system is basically established, the financial administrations keep strong interactions with innovators and the public and jointly build an innovative trail-error-tolerant mechanism that combines rigidity and flexibility, while effectively preventing and resolving financial risks, fully release the potential of financial innovation and development.

5. 2 Financial innovation being more ethical and efficient

Innovation is an inexhaustible source of promoting the FinTech development and an important force to promote the transformation and upgrading of the financial industry. Under the demonstration and leading role of Innovation Regulatory Facility, market entities will more actively use technological means to break the bottleneck of financial development, innovate financial products, re-design business processes, improve service quality and efficiency, and promote the real economy to soar with the "wings" of finance and technology. Through Innovation Regulatory Facility, **financial institutions** can better embrace technology and regulation, accurately grasp the pulse of market and find out the most urgent needs from users, starting from meeting the people's growing needs for a better life, make full use of modern technology to continuously optimize the quality of financial services, improve the accuracy and availability of financial services and make innovation more vital. **Technology companies** continue to strengthen the connection between production and application through Innovation Regulatory Facility, develop in-depth cooperation with financial institutions. Relying on the technical advantages in business systems, computing power storage and algorithm models, technology companies can closely focus on the technological needs in the product development process, accelerate core technology research and development in real financial scenarios, continuously improve adaptability, safety and stability of the technological products.

5.3　Financial services being more beneficial to the people and enterprises

Under the guidance of Innovation Regulatory Facility, financial institutions will better focus on fulfilling the original mission of financial services to the real economy, focus on using technological means to optimize financial service models and enrich the supply of financial products, extend the reach of financial business, cover the "last mile" of inclusive finance, and seamlessly embed financial business into various fields of the real economy, and provide more convenient and inclusive financial services for market entities and the people. **In terms of financial benefits to people**, through Innovation Regulatory Facility, people can actively participate in the FinTech management, make suggestions on financial innovation in terms of business functions, information protection, user experience and risk compensation, etc. , and assist financial services to meet the individualized, diversified and differentiated needs of different customer groups. **In terms of financial benefits to enterprises**, Innovation Regulatory Facility will incubate more high-quality, efficient, safe and convenient financial innovations, and guide market participants to use modern information technologies to reconstruct financial service process, release the value of data production factors, and optimize financial supply in industrial chain and supply chain, allocate financial resources to key areas and weak spots of economic and social development, realize the increase of amount, expansion of scope, improvement of quality and reduction of cost of financing services for all types of enterprises, in particular private, small and micro enterprises, and inject financial vitality into the high-quality development of the real economy.

5. 4   Financial risk control being more precise and effective

Security is the foundation of the healthy development of the financial industry. Preventing and resolving risks in the application of science and technology is essential to maintaining financial stability and economic security. Innovation Regulatory Facility applies new-generation information technology to strengthen risk prevention capabilities, accelerate the exploration of new ways to identify, prevent, and resolve financial risks, and knit a tight "safety net" for financial innovation. **Firstly**, a risk event reporting mechanism covering different market entities and a multi-party risk monitoring platform will be basically established and automated and full-time risk monitoring capabilities will be significantly improved, assisting financial regulation to grasp the overall risk status in a timely and accurate manner, **so as to realize risks being "visible"**. **Secondly**, regulatory knowledge graphs, risk database and construction of regulatory platform will be further advanced. Artificial intelligence, big data and other means will be used to assist financial supervision to look through the covering of multi-level nested business and cross-contagious risks, accurately grasp the substance and key of financial risks, and steadily improve the ability of risk characterization, risk relationship analysis, risk impact assessment, and risk trend research and judgment, **so as to achieve risks being "identifiable"**. **Thirdly**, the coordination mechanism among the public, innovation entities, self-regulatory organizations, and government will be improved step by step. The risk warnings to the financial industry and the society will be timelier. The overall risk control ability and joint handling efficiency will be stably improved. The financial system's ability of risk defense will be comprehensively improved, **so as to ensure risks being "controllable"** .